Advance Praise for *Taste and See*

Like Sue Monk Kidd and Ann Kidd Taylor in *Traveling with Pomegranates*, this mother and daughter tell their interwoven stories in clear, evocative prose, taking us with them from beach to mountain to rural communities and home again. This is a book for both the settled and the seekers, showing us how the multifarious rituals of feeding ourselves and others can nourish, enrich, and change us in unexpected ways. Reading *Taste and See* made me newly alert to the beauty, grace, and serendipity of daily life.

—Jennifer Horne, coeditor of *All Out of Faith: Southern Women on Spirituality and Circling Faith: Southern Women on Spirituality*

This book is so beautiful. Who can't love the idea, the style of writing, the recipes? This is the theology we need, by whatever name. It is down to earth and up to life. Call it poetry, call it music, call it soul food. It fills the body with purpose and pleasure. Taste and see.

—Dr. Jay McDaniel, Professor of Religious Studies, Hendrix College

Since the beginning of the Christian Church, its life has centered on the shared meal. The lasting importance of the Eucharist has shown that meals shared—and the stories shared during those meals—can change lives. For liturgical Christians, the Eucharist is the great Sacrament, but we also realize that all meals are sacramental; what we do as we cook and eat and share stories is a sign of greater connections that we share. In fact, the very acts of cooking and eating and talking with one another brings us together in a mysterious and sacred way.

Taste and See is a worthy contribution to not only cooking, but sacramental theology as well. The "two Joannas" share a love of f a love of cooking, and most importantly, a love of
lives, as a deacon in the church and
have evidenced the power of connec
speak of the potential for restored a

standing over a stove and putting a meal on the table bring us, as we would say in the South.

I have not had such a fun time reading a theologically-oriented cooking book since reading *Supper of the Lamb*. Listen to these stories. Try the recipes. Eat the food and tell your own stories of love and loss. You will find your life changed.

—The Rt. Rev. Larry Benfield, Bishop of Arkansas

I know both of these Joannas. Everyone should be so blessed. They have been woven into my life, and the life of my family over the years, in various places, situations, cities. Theology, in the end, either works or doesn't, based on the experience we have with it in daily life, in the routine, and the ordinary. It becomes real, efficacious, when we can find God in the holy encounters of everyday life. If you struggle with that, this book will get you started.

—The Rt. Rev. Gregory H. Rickel, VIII Bishop of Olympia

Taste and See:

Experiences of God's Goodness Through Stories, Poems, and Food, As Seen by a Mother and Daughter

Joan Seihn

by Joanna E.S. Campbell and the Rev. Joanna J. Seibert, MD

Two Joannas in the Little Room at the Walter Anderson Museum

Taste and See: Experiences of God's Goodness Through Stories, Poems, and Food, As Seen by a Mother and Daughter
© Copyright 2014 Joanna J. Seibert and Joanna E.S. Campbell
All rights reserved.

ISBN: 978-0-9846199-2-4

Cover art by Carla McGoldrick

Proceeds from the sale of *Taste and See* go to Camp Mitchell Episcopal Camp and Conference Center for the Episcopal Church in Arkansas.

Other Temenos Publishing titles by Joanna J. Seibert:
Healing Presence
The Call of the Psalms: A Spiritual Companion for Busy People
The Call of the Psalms: A Spiritual Companion for People in Recovery

Temenos Publishing
www.temenospublishing.com

to our grandmothers Elizabeth, Annie, Florence, and Elizabeth,
and their grandmothers

Table of Contents

Introduction by Joanna E.S. Campbell   01

Comfort Food
Recipe for a Perfect Day   07
Popcorn Theology   08
Joanna's Theological Popcorn Recipe   09
Two Scoops   10
Peppermint Ice Cream in America   12
Food at My Grandparents' Table   15
Mabel's Pound Cake   16
Christmas Eve Chocolate Communion   17
Finding Home in Black-Eyed Peas   19
Dennis' Black-Eyed Pea Recipe   20

Coffee
Coffee with Mary   23
Coffee in Akron   25
Coffee in West Point   26

Breakfast
Breakfast on the Mountain   31
Breakfast with Gay   35
Breakfast with the Osprey   36
Breakfast at Kanuga   37

Guess Who's Coming to Dinner
Family Secrets   41
Mom's Apple Cider   42
Mom's Red Beans and Rice   42
Cooking as a Spiritual Practice   44
Seibert Family Easter Pretzels   48
Arkansas   49
Local Food Dating Leads to God   50
Mabel   55
Mabel's Rolls   55
The Bartender   57
Mealtimes   59

Liminal Cuisine
Skirting the Surf: Beginning a Marriage   63
Morning Meditation   70
Tasting the Present: What I Have Learned from My Daughter   71
Wood Smoked   72
Wood Stained/ Kanuga Toast   76
Recipe for Kanuga Toast   77
The Big Spill   79

The Big Spill a Year Later   83
Gulfshores Three and a Half Years Later   85
Cocktail Harp   86
Praying in Greek   90
Papou's Greek Salad (Hoviatiki)   92
River Food   93
Menu for a 100-Mile Race   99
Lunch on Your Personal Day, The Next Right Thing   102

There is Room for Everyone at the Table

The Spiritual Meaning of Delicious   107
How I Got Over Being a Radical Foodie Southern Health Nut   110
Dennis' Re-Sanctified Cornbread Recipe   113
Prayers of Thanksgiving   114
Revolving Tables Restaurant   116
Two Parties at Children's Hospital   118
Mothering Tea: My New Life As a Priest's Wife   120
Joanna's Oatmeal Chocolate Chip Cookie Recipe   123
Clams and Other Mysteries   125
Kinds of Prayer   130

Acknowledgments   131

Introduction

When I moved to Petit Jean Mountain in 2007, I came with scales fixed onto my eyes. I arrived with a broken heart, having left a village in rural New Brunswick, Canada, a place that offered what I had been longing for in ways of living in community. I expected Petit Jean, Arkansas, the land and the people on the mountain, to mirror these elements, just as I had experienced across the border. My expectations were high. I was continually disappointed by the differences and didn't miss an opportunity to share my frustrations.

A neighbor on the mountain listened patiently to my rants. Ed is a sheep farmer, and my respect for him runs deep, with his years of dedication to community and agricultural sustainability. A farmer never stops working, and yet, anytime I stopped by the red barn on my way home from work, Ed was available for a chat. Often, he would excitedly share the products of a new cooperative farming endeavor. One autumn afternoon, I stopped by the red barn where Ed invited me to the picnic table to taste sheep's milk cheese that a friend had made with the milk of his sheep. It was divine. We sipped lemonade and tasted samples of the cheese with drops of honey. As we enjoyed these simple delights, I began my list of complaints about the lack of sustainable community on Petit Jean, in Arkansas…the United States of America. Ed listened intently, and then something amazing happened. He offered a reality check about my recent move to Arkansas. He said, "Joanna, first of all, what you're describing sounds like a pretty lonely place to be. This angst you're feeling sounds like a heavy burden that you've been carrying around for months. Look around you. Sustainability is in the eye of the beholder. Elements of sustainable community are around us all the time. It's a matter of opening our eyes and accessing it." Wow. I could feel the scales falling from my eyes, and by some kind of grace, I felt God opening my heart in a new way.

Food is our common denominator. Sharing meals has the power to distract us from our worries and set our eyes on what is important, if only for a brief moment. These are moments of grace where we are able to truly taste and see that God is good, and sharing meals is often a medium for these simple and profound moments. These interactions are seeds that begin to slowly germinate, helping us to see how we are all connected and how we are held in the palm of God's hand. Sharing food carries an unexpected power and can be a surprising pathway for experiencing what some call the Beloved Community and what others may describe as the Kingdom of God.

Taste and See offers stories, poems, and recipes from two women in two different generations: a mother and daughter with the same name, sharing their life experiences in tasting and seeing the goodness of God. I am the daughter. The idea for this book began when my mother was a child sitting at her grandparents' table and tasting home-cooked meals, sharing in the comfort of good food and unconditional love. The idea continued forward when my mother chose to stop cooking when I was a child, marking those infrequent moments of baking bread together as sacred treasures. The idea sprang forth abundantly when I moved back to Arkansas, and my mother and I began a new kind of food, community, and agriculture relationship. We hosted book groups on food culture, picked seeds out of cotton for planting in a demonstration garden, and we shoveled soil and compost together for a community garden between two churches in Little Rock.

All of the stories here in some way involve food as a vehicle for expressing the goodness of God. These stories are celebrations. They are confessional, and they are prayers and reminders for the simplicity of food and fellowship.

Our unspoken bias is the need for connection with others in our spiritual journey. In certain ways, sharing food is an act of bravery because we engage in a mutual vulnerability. These are openings for seeing God in each other. It can be awkward, difficult, and messy at times. Community is messy. Family and friendships are messy. I have had numerous experiences of the Divine, of the goodness of God: in solitary excursions, in the mountains of western Montana and in the woods behind my childhood home. This book is *not* about experiencing the goodness of God alone on a mountaintop. These are stories of reaching out, sometimes beyond our comfort zones—in connection with each other in coffee shops, Parish halls, restaurants, home kitchens, front porches, hospitals, and dining rooms.

My mother is a pediatric radiologist and has been an Episcopal deacon for eleven years. She has been involved in the established church for most of her seventy years. She has seen the goodness of God most especially in music, in her work, in difficult times with the sick and dying, but also in her everyday life. I am in my thirties and have kept a journal most of my life. I have experienced God in my writing and in my love of nature, community, and the outdoors. Only recently I have become more involved to the established church when a year ago I married an Episcopal priest. I bring back to the church my life experiences of God in the outdoors in China, Montana, Canada, Arkansas, and now Seattle. I have been especially involved in experiential learning and food sustainability.

The book is divided into six sections with stories either by my mother (JJS) or me (JESC), sometimes followed by a poem or a recipe. Often the story by one leads to a story by the other. The stories in the first section called **Comfort Food** are all about experiences where food

2

brought to mind a comfortable and nurturing experience. *Coffee* is stories of experiences talking to friends over coffee. *Breakfast* describes experiences by either my mother or me at breakfast. *Guess Who's Coming to Dinner* shares experiences of more unusual meals. *Liminal Cuisine* describes physical and spiritual edge-world experiences of God in meals. *There is Room for Everyone at the Table* is stories of unexpected abundance and hopefulness and the insights that emerge when we are outside our comfort zones.

—Joanna E. S. Campbell

Comfort Food

Recipe for a Perfect Day

Begin morning with writing in your favorite overstuffed chair.
Enjoy peppermint tea and porridge.
Stare out the window to the garden, the downtown skyline, Puget
Sound, and the Olympic mountains.
Write a little more.
Share a butternut squash pizza with Dennis.
Slowly eat the brick-oven baked crust.
Read fiction until you fall asleep.
Wake in the late afternoon to the sound of light rain.
Honor the impulse to visit the used bookstore, the one with all the cats.
Leave with armloads of books.
Celebrate happy hour at The Grotto.
Share garlic fries and fancy appetizers with Dennis.
Return home at dusk.
Read fiction until you fall asleep.

—JESC

Popcorn Theology

Walk inside my parent's home any night of the week and you are bound to smell freshly popped popcorn. Enter the rectory where I live, and one of the first things you'll see is our red popcorn machine adorned with various oils, utensils, and varieties of corn. My husband, Dennis, agreed a well-made popcorn machine was a good start to our marriage.

Churches have artifacts, which are physical objects located throughout the sanctuary. They are objects with a story and purpose. For some, the purpose is rooted in liturgical tradition. For others, the objects emerged out of a particular circumstance, like the time a parishioner underwent jaw surgery, couldn't sip the communion wine, and so was offered a silver straw to sip from. The silver straw remained on the altar alongside the other communion vessels for years. People forgot its original story, but the artifact became the sacred, sterling silver straw.

In many homes, televisions are positioned in such a way resembling a shrine, indicating *this* is the most important object in the house. Dennis and I don't have a television; we have a popcorn machine. Popcorn is an artifact in my family. It's something I take for granted every day. It is a practice that has many stories of origin, some of which I know. I jokingly tell friends that eating popcorn is one of my spiritual disciplines, and my mom is my original mentor.

For fun, I gave my mom a rubber popcorn ball that I found in a children's toy store. The popcorn ball sat on my mom's desk for years along with her books on spiritual journeys. When the ball went missing, my mom wrote a note to Faith, who cleans their house once a week. I saw the piece of paper with my mom's handwriting on top of the microwave. "Faith, there was a popcorn ball on my desk. I can't find it. Please see if you can find it. Thanks." The popcorn ball eventually turned up, though it was deflated. The lumpy ball still sits on my mom's desk.

Years ago, if you were a new visitor to St. Margaret's Episcopal Church, you would have been greeted with bags of popcorn. St. Margaret's began as a mission in a west Little Rock movie theater. Movie posters and popcorn became part of the new church's DNA. Years later in their beautifully constructed church, St. Margaret's hit a rough patch in leadership, with members beginning to stray. Dennis claimed the popcorn machine needed to come out of the storage closet and to "get the smell of popcorn back into the building."

When Dennis was hospitalized for five weeks in ICU with a life-threatening illness, he was unconscious for most of the time. For me, living in a hospital for several weeks produces an inadvertent daily rhythm. Wake, pray, yogurt, juice, pray, listen, be still, eat popcorn, pray some more. Popcorn is one of the few foods I can stomach when I'm stressed. Popcorn and prayer brought comfort through hours and days of medical uncertainty.

Maybe it is because of the state I was born in: Iowa. Perhaps the rolling cornfields imprinted themselves on my infant spirit. I have read about the perils of genetic modification and seen films like *King Corn* that depict the mess our country is in for how we treat the land and farmers. There are ways to source locally. Organic is always an option at my food co-op. I could be a more responsible popcorn consumer. Sometimes I can't resist the coconut oil-laden popcorn in our Seattle movie theaters. Sometimes I just need an hour or two in a darkened room where the present moment includes an uncomplicated, lightly salted pleasure.

Taste and see that God is good.
—JESC

Joanna's Theological Popcorn Recipe
My favorite way to cook popcorn is in a big pot on the stovetop. I like to mix various oils that are suited for high heat and add complex flavors.

½ cup of popcorn kernels
1 Tbsp. Grapeseed Oil
1 Tbsp. Almond Oil
1 tsp. of Walnut and/or Sesame oil

Mix the oils in the pot and heat to Med/High. Place the kernels in the pot, and partly cover the pot with a lid, so steam may escape. When the kernels begin popping, gently shake the pot to prevent the kernels from burning.

Toppings I like:
Sea salt
Truffle salt
Drizzled flax oil instead of butter
Brewer's yeast

Two Scoops

Today I give thanks that I may have seen a glimpse of the reflected face of God. We are on the Alabama Gulf Coast in Foley and stop at Stacey's Old Tyme Drug Store on Laurel Street. This corner drug store is a wonderful step back in time with a soda fountain and friendly hometown faces.

Stacey's reminds me of Riddle's, the drug store in my small hometown in Virginia that I walked to every day after school. Two stores up from Riddle's was my grandfather's jewelry store, where I would first stop to receive a nickel from my grandfather to buy an ice cream cone. In Stacey's there is an old time jukebox and a player piano along the walls that frame the front of the store filled with metal ice cream tables and chairs. To one side is a large metal box filled with cold bottled drinks. Behind the long marble counter and in front of the sparkling traditional drug store mirror stands John, the "Fizzsician," the most friendly, most positive person I have encountered in some time. His cheerfulness, his caring for his customers, his striving for excellence in his shakes and sodas, and his reasonable prices are beyond comparison.

Observing someone who seems to love his work and loves people is like going to a museum to study a priceless work of art. We go there not only for a "shake fix" but also for a "feel good fix." John makes you feel good. He seems to love life and love people—all kinds of people. As he takes your ice cream order, he makes eye contact and acts as if each of us is his only customer. He brightens your day with his big smile and upbeat remarks. "Welcome back to Foley. Isn't the weather great today." He hands you a napkin and glass of ice water before he takes your order. "Our special today is the peach ice cream. One scoop or two? Cup or cone? Sit at our counter or a table and rest awhile." He makes you stop, rest, and look on the brighter side of life. He challenges you to lighten up, not be so serious. Of course he is the supreme extrovert, constantly talking, but even we introverts want to catch a little of what he has to offer—and it is more than a wonderful milkshake. His cheerful voice and smile are infectious. We always leave in a better frame of mind.

Observing John makes you realize what a difference one person can make in the attitude of a whole town, what a difference one person can make by blooming where he is planted, what a difference one person can make by reaching out in love to others in his own unique way, what a difference a person can make by his positive attitude in a job that many people would think mundane and uninteresting and unchallenging. Jungian friends tell me that someone I greatly admire may represent a shadow figure—a part of me that is under-developed but there for the asking. Today as I leave Stacey's Drug Store I take with me in my mind a wonderful role model with attributes of kindness, cheerfulness, and an unbelievable positive outlook on life. This image I saw reflected in the drug store mirror seems to fit one of "the many faces of God" my daughter and I have encountered in this walk we are taking together through these stories. How exciting to meet that image face-to-face. Tonight as I review the day, I give thanks for the unique opportunity to be with a role model who has something I want to have in my life as well.

Taste and see that God is good.
—JJS

Stacey's

At the counter being served
by the Fizzsician

Peppermint Ice Cream in America

As I walk through the Student Center at the University of Montana, my potter friend, Hal, leads me to a photograph of Bohemian Waxwings perched on snowy branches. There are at least a dozen dotting the picture with their brilliant yellow, black, white, and beige. A vague thought occurs that part of the reason for their clustering is to generate warmth...as a community. Fundamental as hunger and equally mysterious, "community" has held me captive since I can remember. There is a subterranean flow within that calls out for expression, to act out and form connections with the people, the land I find myself on. It is easy enough to make friends wherever I go. These are my individual, isolated pockets of community dispersed across the continent and the globe. But what of this community that lives in one place, a group of people who work and play together, who have an ethos grounded in the greater good and recognition of interdependence?

These waxwings remind me of how disconnected we have become. Fighting an evolutionary biology of living in small groups where each person is honored and respected for their gifts and usefulness, I now puzzle over the *zing* that runs through my body in the infrequent, unexpected times of being part of something meaningful with others. Hal points out their lines and color, the simplicity of their beauty. "They're so cheerful and unconcerned with all of the worries we seem to have," he says.

Hal is my dad's age and has a daughter around my age. He wanted to be part of her life, but that wasn't an option. He never really looked like a dad to me or that he could be *my* dad. Going grey for him meant his curly fire-red hair turning blonde. His hands, his hands are amazing. They are large, broad, and thick from handling slabs of porcelain clay, throwing pots, thumbing and pressing and kneading for hours. A free spirit who would've been content if the 1960s never ended, he's a bachelor in the ultimate with many a tale of whirlwind romances and broken hearts peppered throughout the state.

"Hey kiddo. You want some ice cream?" We sit on his porch with the shade of Norway maples and his hanging geranium baskets. The Big Dipper peppermint ice cream is perfection, and he shares stories from the past. Old girl friends, escapades from working at the mental health center, the days growing up in Bozeman, hitchhiking across the country with a friend who couldn't run fast enough for moving trains, how they had to run like crazy to catch a ride with a truck full of bee hives, dodging the draft by enrolling in grad school, the time in his 20s when he was just a greenbuck-writer working the beat on the local paper, how he overcame agoraphobia in the Big Sky state. He has so many stories, and I can't get enough of them. The scent of fresh-baked bread rises from the bakery below to his second story apartment. He shares a haiku with me that he's just written. "I'm putting a little book together," he says, "and I wrote something as if we were together."

There's my girlfriend's bike
Locked to mine against the fence
'spose they'll have a trike?

Hal tells me community is a place connected to our identity— community is shaped by how a person sees the world, what you need, what you are looking for. The very nature of my history with a place makes me a part of that place. "You *are* part of the Missoula scene," he says.

It's said that in the valleys of western Montana, newcomers settle down because of the wildness of the place, and they end up staying because of the people. In a state where homes and towns are strewn across a rocky, raw land populated by bears, lions, and deer, community is a state of mind.

I hug my knees and keep thinking of Paul Simon's *American Tune*, how much his words resonate, how I don't seem to know what home is anymore.

"I don't have a friend who feels at ease. I don't know a dream that's not been shattered or driven to its knees."

Hal invites me inside to watch old movies. His home is decorated with his pottery—vases, bowls, and mugs adorned with line drawings of flute playing, fruit eating, tea-drinking muses. For his 60th birthday, we decided I'd pretend I was his long-lost cousin, Joanna from Texarkana. I pulled up as thick a Southern accent as I possibly could, and to this day, people from that party are convinced of our bloodline.

Maybe Hal is inviting me to hold this notion of community more gently, to be careful in the politic judgments. I am beginning to wonder if the sole purpose of life is to be continually cracked and broken open for all creation to see in order to keep learning, stretching—flying far, far beyond the little realities we've lassoed.

Someone, a long time ago, decided to name waxwings Bohemians, a bird whose survival depends on huddling together, working together, without which there would be no colors to name or beauty to marvel. Despite planet-altering practices by humans, nature continues to offer wisdom, lessons that can help me remember something. Something about being part of nature, the land, and each other. Something about how to relate to one another. A memory that knew itself before I knew the world. I want to remember. I ache for this remembrance.

What are the colors of our plumage? How do we re-remember? How do we build from fragment? Perhaps remembering something we never knew in the first place? These are the questions that can become demons if I'm not careful.

I now live in a place called Petit Jean Mountain, in my home state of Arkansas, and I haven't been back to Montana for two years. No more porch talks and ice cream with Hal. But I keep thinking of the picture he showed me. I've never seen a Bohemian Waxwing here either, but each spring I pay the fee to explore the swamps of eastern Arkansas. I'm looking for the Lord God bird, the Ivory Billed, a bird we thought was forgotten, erased from the planet. In a beat-up canoe surrounded by a forest of bald cypress and swarms of heat-loving dragon flies, my belly tingles at the thought of seeing that red crest and those unashamed eyes. I keep paddling, and I remember the words my friend, Ragan, shared with me. He says we get into trouble when we focus so much on the self, even in landscapes. Being on the land, there is a surrendering that can take place. He invites me to surrender judgments. Surrender to place. Community begins with a state of mind. Perhaps it's time for some ice cream with friends.

Taste and see that God is good.
—JESC

Food at My Grandparents' Table

The dreaded call comes late at night. "Your grandfather is in a coma. We think he had a stroke." In the morning I board the first plane back to my hometown of Tidewater, Virginia to visit him.

Thoughts flood my mind on the long plane ride. My grandfather was the most significant person in my growing-up years. I spent every Sunday afternoon and evening with him and my grandmother. We ate the same Sunday dinner: corn bread, fried chicken, green beans, potato salad, and Mabel's (my grandparents' cook) homemade pound cake. After dinner I would sit on his knee as he read me the funny papers. We all then took a short nap. I can still see him and my grandmother lying together on the small couch in their dining room/den. Then we would go to the country to his farm, walking the length of his property by the Mattaponi and York Rivers as he told me stories about his growing-up days. Sometimes we would visit his nearby relatives and the cemetery where my grandmother's parents are buried. Then we'd walk to his townhouse for Sunday night church, 7-up floats, and the *Ed Sullivan* show. I would spend the night in their big guest room bed and then walk to school the next day.

My grandfather is a symbol of unconditional love, always there for me, supporting and loving me in good times and bad. I did not spend much time with him after I left my hometown and went away to college and medical school. He, however, never forgot me and sent me letters every week on his 30-year-old typewriter with intermittent keys that barely print. Every other sentence ended with *etc, etc, etc.* Each letter was filled with stories of his experiences away from home in World War I and words of love and encouragement. Always enclosed was a dollar bill. When he suffered this stroke twenty years later, I am devastated. I cannot bear to lose the love which I knew he showed to me no matter what I had done.

I walk into my grandfather's hospital room for the first time. There is an immediate look of astonishment on his face. I believe he knows me even though he never again shows any sign of recognition. As I sit by his bed and listen to his labored breathing, I feel helpless. What can I do? All my years of medical practice do not give me answers. I remember his faith tradition and honor it by reading the Psalms aloud, beginning with Psalm 1

On his law, they meditate day and night.

They are like trees planted by streams of water,
Which yield their fruit in its season,
And their leaves do not wither.

I am embarrassed when personnel come into the room, but an inner voice says this is what my grandfather wants to hear. I am calmed. This is what I would want at my deathbed—to hear the Psalms read by someone who loves me.

My grandfather's illness and death become a major turning point in my life. This is the beginning of my journey in earnest seeking to find a connection with a power greater than myself. I desperately want to believe that somehow I will stay connected to my grandfather, and my tradition tells me this might be possible through a belief in a God. I cannot bear the thought of never again knowing the love I received from my grandfather. I want to return to my tradition and begin a new spiritual journey. My grandfather's unconditional love leads me back to the unconditional love of a God. I learn from my grandfather about "trees planted together by streams of water," hoping to bear fruit in our season where " leaves do not wither."

And it all started with cornbread every Sunday dinner.

Taste and see that God is good.
—JJS

Mabel's Pound Cake
3 cups of sugar
3 ½ cups of flour (sifted)
2 tsp. vanilla
5 eggs
1 tsp. baking powder
½ lb. butter
2 Tbsp. hot water
¼ tsp. salt

Cream butter and sugar. Add eggs and water. Add flour, salt and vanilla. Beat until very smooth. Bake in greased and floured tube pan. Cook slowly a reasonable length of time. (1 hour at 350 degrees)

Christmas Eve Chocolate Communion

The bare-footed tiny angels with their silver tinseled halos and shiny white gowns have all fluttered and twirled up and down St. Luke's Episcopal Church aisles as "This is My Dancing Day" is played on the harp. As the Christmas Eve pageant progresses the youngest angels add in an extra two-step dance back and forth between the steps to the altar where baby Jesus is resting and their parents' pews. Next appear brown robed little shepherd boys processing down the center aisle to see the baby Jesus. The clank, clank of their shepherds' staffs that look more like adult walking canes are almost in rhythm with the violinist playing "What Child Is This?" No live baby Jesus this year, just a doll. Actually, our administrator named her, "Scary Doll." Her mouth is wide open like a bird, and she is obviously a blue-eyed girl doll, well wrapped and lying in the traditional manger that has been used in so many other Christmas pageants before, by history, fifty-seven counting this year. Teenaged Mary and Joseph try to comfort and quiet the shepherds and angels as the story of Jesus' nativity is read by older youth dressed in white choir robes. I-phones, flash photography, and videos are in abundance as proud parents and grandparents search for their special shepherds and angels. Max sweetly sings unaccompanied the last verse of "Once in Royal David's City" as the pageant ends, and our rector goes and sits with the children on the chancel steps.

He pulls out a tray of chocolate pieces. He passes the tray around and asks each child, "What does the chocolate candy look like?"

"Square, dark brown," words are heard.

"Does anyone know where chocolate comes from?"

"The candy store," is the best answer.

Carey then tells them that the rough leathery rinds of the tropically grown cocoa beans are removed, and the beans are then fermented, roasted, and ground until they liquefy into what is called cocoa butter and cocoa solid. He then reads the long list of ingredients in the Christmas candy written in small print on the bottom of the chocolate bar's gold tin container: sugar, milk cocoa butter, chocolate, soy lecithin, vanillin, and artificial flavor. He asks, "Do any of you know what chocolate is like by learning about its ingredients, what stuff is in it, where it came from, or where it was made?"

Heads shake "No."

"Yes, only by experiencing chocolate, by eating it, do we know what chocolate really is."

All of the children eagerly agree with him, and each then receives a generous piece of dark imported chocolate. I hear several "Yumms" and "more."

Carey then asks the children, "Is eating rich chocolate similar to the story of Jesus' being born into the world? We can learn about God in books, in pictures, in writings, even hear about God from other people, but only when we experience God ourselves, do we really know God."

Christmas is God's offer to each of us to experience in the flesh, and

Taste and see that God is good.
—JJS

St. Luke's priest, Carey Stone, giving chocolate to angels and shepherds on Christmas Eve

Finding Home in Black-Eyed Peas

I didn't realize I was a Southerner until I moved to Seattle three years ago. The moment crystallized in the Safeway on Rainier Avenue while I circled aisles in search of cornmeal and collard greens. A friendly clerk led me to the appropriate section: Ethnic. There amongst Matzo crackers and Hoisin sauce were the Southern staples so common in my hometown. As a Caucasian female, I attended Little Rock Central High School with a different label: Minority. In the span of twenty years, I have puddle-jumped labels: privileged minority to spiritual-but-not-religious to clergy spouse. In Seattle, the foods I know from Arkansas are lumped into one murky label, and finding these ingredients under such a non-descriptive title feels like witnessing the blending of hundreds of years of family stories and recipes. I have a theory that delicious, home-cooked meals are birthed in the privacy of steamy kitchens dotted from the Mississippi River Delta to the Ozarks. I can only begin to imagine the stories, both heart-lifting and soul-stirring, within the homes of my neighbors.

A friend in Seattle went looking for black-eyed peas yesterday. She, like so many of us, enjoys preparing the traditional New Year's Day dish, whose legend holds the promise of prosperity for the coming year. The peas represent coins, and if you're on top of Southern culinary traditions, you'll prepare greens, symbolizing cash, to serve alongside the peas. Her search turned into a wild goose chase. She eventually found them at Bob's Quality Meats, a place Southerners know they can find boudin and whole hogs ready to smoke in a neighborhood called Columbia City. (Columbia City also bears the label of most-diverse-zip-code in the United States, with a minimum of fifty-nine spoken languages). My husband, Dennis, often says, "I can live just about anywhere as long as it has a good kitchen." Seattle has the added benefit of fresh ingredients within walking distance of our house.

Moving to Seattle forced me to ask questions about who and what I am. I've made many places outside the South my home, all rural for the most part. It wasn't until an urban corner of the Pacific Northwest became my home that I realized how challenging it is putting words to such dynamic, cultural characteristics. Not only is Arkansas a melting pot of ethnicities and traditions, but it is also a place of ironies and welcome happenstance. Add to the mix a relational way of being, and you have a distinct creation: 1) people who aren't afraid to start up conversation with ease, which leads to the revelation that you never meet a stranger in Arkansas, and 2) you never know what new, delightfully unexpected surprise you're going to stumble upon, and believe me, it's a guarantee this will happen to you. The cuisine is one of many manifestations of this phenomenon. It may be crispy bacon served in your Bloody Mary or pineapple cilantro popsicles from the farmer's market. Perhaps it's Thai-style shrimp over Arkansas-grown Basmati rice. Or maybe it is grilled catfish with smoked poblano peppers. Today, in my family, it's black-eyed peas and cornbread made in a cast-iron skillet seasoned with flax oil.

When Dennis and I returned from a New Year's Eve dinner, he began soaking the peas while my nieces and I watched the ball drop in New York City. The smells of sautéed onions and bell peppers roused me from sleep the next morning. I can't think of a better way to welcome the new year. I found Dennis stirring the bubbling pot, and I could see the little peas dancing on the surface. "Ooooo, that looks good. When will it be ready?"

"Soon," he said, "Very soon."

Dennis sprinkles sweet onions and Louisiana hot sauce over the peas. I dip my spoon into the steaming bowl. *Tastes like home*, I think. For the moment, home is standing in my parent's kitchen in Little Rock, Arkansas. For the moment, home is the taste of cornbread and spicy black-eyed peas. I lick the bowl clean, full with prosperity.

Taste and see that God is good.
—JESC

Dennis' Black-Eyed Pea Recipe
1 pound of dried black-eyed peas. If you don't live near Bob's Quality Meats, most major grocery stores carry them.
1 bell pepper
2 stalks of celery
1 medium-sized yellow onion
2 Tbsp. of mined garlic
1 quart of chicken broth (or water if vegetarian)
1 hamhock (optional)
2 cups of white wine
Ground black pepper
Cajun seasoning

Soak black-eyed peas overnight in a salty water brine. Make brine with a quarter cup of sea salt with a gallon of water. Chop bell pepper, celery, and onion. In a large Dutch oven, sauté the pepper, celery, and onion together until the onions are clear. Add garlic last. Add chicken broth to the sauté. Drain and rinse the black-eyed peas and add to the vegetable mix. Add the hamhock. Finish with white wine until there is an inch of liquid above the peas. Season with ground black pepper and Cajun spices to your liking.

Coffee

Coffee with Mary

Two weeks after her daughter's funeral, I met Mary for coffee. Anne had been killed in a tragic train accident in another country the summer before she was to enter college. It was an usually cool summer morning. I felt Mary's presence in the restaurant before I even saw her. After a tearful hug we ordered our coffee and immediately began talking about Anne's funeral. We marveled at the number of friends Anne had and the people she had touched in her young life. We went over all the details of the glorious celebration of Anne's life: the music, the choir, the liturgy, the reception and how no one wanted to leave. Mary then began slowly to talk about the new directions she already felt in her life. She told me how she had spent much time trying not to wear masks in her life, but that this great loss had made her even more desiring of not being anything that was false to her. She was living her life one day at a time. She was not making a lot of plans and was trying to be open to what God had in store for her that day. She also had a vision of what her life's mission should be: to become the person God had intended her to be with all her heart. Mary was not certain what that was, but she was more open than she ever had known. She spoke of feeling God's presence and support throughout this entire tragedy. She wondered how anyone could survive such a loss without the love and faith in God. Then she could barely speak as she softly whispered that she had some insight into the thoughts of our Lord's mother, another Mary, at the cross. Mary then looked away from me and at the cars passing by in the busy street close to our table. As we sat in silence, I could not help being overwhelmed with thoughts of how awful the loss of a child must be. It is unimaginable. Parents should not have to bury their children. My mind filled with images of parents of children I have known in my work at Children's Hospital who have sat by bedsides as their children have suffered and died. There was love, protection, caring, sorrow, anger, comfort, helplessness, and surrender, as I have never seen in any other situations.

Mary's eyes once again met mine, and I was overwhelmed with the love and faith that shone back from within. She set down her coffee cup and held out her hand and took mine in hers, enveloping mine with her warmth.

Even in times of great tragedy,

Taste and see that God is good.
—JJS

Anne

Coffee in Akron

I repeatedly receive calls from a radiologist at a Children's Hospital about coming to Akron, Ohio to come and speak about work I have done with children with Sickle Cell Disease. I am trying to cut back on the busyness of my life and keep refusing. I don't want to go to Akron, Ohio. I feel like Jonah being called to Nineveh. I often go to a 12-step meeting at noon where there is a picture of the home in Akron of Dr. Bob Smith, one of the founders of the 12-step recovery program. I keep seeing that small brick-fronted house every day as I keep getting calls from the physician in Akron. I finally wonder if this just may be a message to go to Akron. I call back and say I will go on the condition that they will take me to Dr. Bob's house. Of course none of my hosts have heard of Dr. Bob. I go and Akron is a wonderful town that I almost missed seeing. I stay in a delightful hotel with rooms restructured from rounded silos that once were used for grain storage. I also think I was able to help one of the children there with Sickle Cell Disease. After the lectures I am taken to Dr. Bob's house, 855 Admore Avenue, modest, easily missed, tucked away in a quiet neighborhood. I sit at the kitchen table and drink coffee where Dr. Bob met with people seeking recovery from alcoholism. I go upstairs to the small bedroom where Dr. Bob met with Bill Wilson, a stock speculator from New York, on the day after Mother's Day in 1935. In this sparsely furnished upper room these two men eventually began a program, before I was born, to save my life and the lives of so many more. This is the work of God who is on our side. This is the God of my understanding: someone who loves us so dearly that there is a plan to care for and save us before we are born. Sitting in that house was one of the most powerful spiritual experiences I have known. I have an overwhelming sense of God's love for me and each of us manifested through two men I have never known but now want to remember.

Taste and see that God is good.
—JJS

Dr. Bob's House in Akron Ohio

Coffee in West Point

Visiting your childhood home where you were born and reared can be one of life's most bittersweet paradoxes—anticipation of a place that has stood still in your memory—realization that it has changed and you have changed—hope for healing of memories. I still well remember making that monumental trip just before my mother gave up our childhood home. I slept in my old bed for the last time and went through all my parent's possessions to choose which material memories I wanted to keep. I walked the streets I took to school, had one last visit by the river running by my home, rode a bicycle down "back street," and sat one last time in the choir stalls in the Methodist church where I was nurtured. I talked to an old girlfriend as if it had only been an hour since we last spoke. I saw a man who had been a star athlete and my idol when I was in high school. I still remember the number of his basketball jersey: forty-four.

Sometimes the nostalgia was too much and I had to break away. Indeed, I did come home early, partly because the experience was too intense. I talked to saints, everyday people who are angels unaware—most of whom I saw with new eyes on this last visit. I saw "ordinary people" who knew secrets I still haven't learned: a ninety-one-year-old neighbor who has battled a fractured hip and breast cancer and still walks every day to the drugstore at nine each morning to have a cup of coffee with a friend who formerly lived next door; another neighbor who cares for a ninety-three-year-old neighbor in a nursing home whose only relative, her sixty-year-old son, is a street person in New York; a next door neighbor with a heart of gold who cried when we left; a widower, a recovering alcoholic, whose life has been transformed by caring for animals and small children; the mother of a high school friend whose health is failing, who spends most of the year with her daughter out-of-state, but returns to her home at least a few weeks each year to "feel her roots;" a woman physician who gave her marriage and family a high priority and who has become one of the most nurturing physicians I know in an age where it has been more acceptable for women to be objective, focused, and masculine. For me she is a role model of a woman succeeding in her work using feminine values of relationship. I am still amazed by the serendipity that we met "by chance" at the post office on this last visit. I am constantly amazed by the way God works—throwing people in my path I need to see and learn from—if I will only see them or take time to talk to them.

I saw others who are models for a life I fear. I know how easily they got there—the pain of life on life's terms was too great to bear. My prayer for you and me today is that God will let us see when we are on that path, may we see the light in that darkness, and may our wounds be healed with God's tears: the alcoholic who only leaves her home once a week to go to the beauty parlor; the businesswoman who awakens at five in the morning each day so she won't have to dream and deal with her dreams; the couple whose only relationship in their marriage is convenience.

The miracle of life is the ordinary—the ordinary people in my small hometown who know everyone else's business but who also know what reaching out to others and caring is all about. The tragedy of life is also the ordinary—those who have retreated or escaped from life's everydayness because of the pain. Life is painful, sometimes unbearable. What turns us into survivors and lovers? The difference may be that the lovers and survivors seem to be living a life of gratitude where they daily *taste and see that God is good.*

—JJS

Breakfast

Breakfast on the Mountain

It is Sunday morning, and it's the perfect day to get struck by lightning. There are no prior engagements, no last-minute proposals to write, or conflicts to diffuse. I am lost in dreaming, lounging in flannel pajamas, considering bathing but not taking the thought too seriously. I savor cornbread with cranberries and toasted pecans and drink in rich English novels. I eat and read and write and stare into space while slipping into corners of my mind begging for trouble. Perfection.

Accented throughout the morning are the staccato thunderstorms releasing their weight in water, rumbling the sky over my home at the edge of Petit Jean Mountain. All is right with the world, and yet my heart pounds for something more.

I close my eyes and see myself standing in tall grass tickling my calves and picking sun-ripened raspberries under a sky full of soft, punchy cumuli at the place called Salmon Beach. In my mind, I walk the point at Fort Morgan amidst a city of birds and an oil rig-dotted horizon. There is the place where I can take afternoon naps in the home made by farmer hands, where I let myself be tucked away behind miles of red clay roads, national forest, and rogue boars. I want to slowly kiss the men I know who work with their hands—slowly, slowly kiss from a burning place inside, a place from every atom of my body. My heart pounds for an authentic life in a home reflecting years of staying put, grounded, connected to a place. Staying put is the novelty late-night body hunger. It's a new kind of seduction, and I am learning about what this means. Staying put in the South has always been a lover just out of reach. Today should be enough. And then the sky offers a whole new kind of big wet kiss.

Washing my breakfast bowl in the kitchen sink, I stare out the window to the lush green forest soaking up the raindrops. In my dreaming, I suddenly feel the house shake as a large crack unfurls overhead. "This is going to land close," I think, and in a matter of seconds while picture frames slam onto the floor, I see a lightning bolt strike an oak tree one hundred feet in front of me. Dropping the bowl into the sink with the water running, my hands shake as a tingling sensation dances from my toes up through my body. A ball of white, pink, and lavender fire bursts forth. A plume of white smoke billows from the side of the house. My eyes are wide open.

As I run through the house expecting to see the surrounding forest burst into flames while my house melts from an electrical fire, I realize several things. The Volunteer Fire Department will be here as soon as I call them, I have a sink full of dirty dishes, my bed is unmade, and I'm wearing baby blue flannel sock monkey pajamas.

The black soot around the phone jack tells me the landlines are fried. Thank goodness for the work cell my boss insisted on despite my resistance to that kind of technology. As I cradle the phone in my neck, I attempt, with great difficulty, to change out of the pajamas into something more respectable—blue jeans and a wool sweater. It's about ninety-five degrees outside, even in the deluge that turns my front yard into perfect rice paddy habitat.

I know there is something wrong when a pleasant voice on the end of the line says, "411 Information."

No, no, no, I scream in my head. I need the Fire Department, not Information.

I quickly enter the correct numbers for 911, and before the dispatcher can ask me what my emergency is, words spill out in forced, clear determination. "I live at 1938 Petit Jean Mountain Road. There was a lightning strike and there is smoke coming out from the side of the house. Please send help."

As if she has all the time in the world, she asks, "Ma'am, what county do you live in?"

Excuse me? I don't have time to discuss this. "Conway County."

"Please hold, ma'am. I will connect you with that dispatcher."

"What?"

"911. What is your emergency?" I go through the drill again. This time, the voice tells me to get out of the house immediately. Help is on the way.

I quickly get over the vanity about my unmade bed though I do run into the kitchen to throw a tea towel over the sink. Ridiculous. A thought quickly runs through my head that this is the kind of scenario people are asked about all the time. This is the situation life coaches pose as a way to inspire individuals and gain perspective. *If your house were on fire, and you could remove only one item, what would it be?*

The answer is clear. "I don't have time to think about that. Get the hell out of the house. Now."

This leads me to now believe that sort of questioning is pure romanticism, a luxury.

Dressed for a winter's day, my glasses immediately fog up as I dash out the front door, slosh through the front yard, and seek cover inside the wood shed. Within seconds, I can't tell the difference between the sweat pouring out of my body and the warm rain soaking through. Standing under the shed, I shift my weight back and forth for a bit as if I'm about to wet my pants, and it suddenly occurs to me that I'm standing under a tin roof.

I leap from under the shed into my Subaru Forester. Isn't it true that the rubber tires will protect me? The eight minutes it takes for the First Responder to arrive feels like an eternity. Helplessness washes over me as I watch my house and wonder what is happening in the inner walls.

Is an electrical fire a slow burn, or do things start exploding? Do I need to be far away in case of heat radiation? Does the Volunteer Fire Department know where I live?

Lightning continues to bounce around the mountain, and I begin to feel like I'm at the center of an electric globe that shoots out purple and blue streaks.

I see headlights through the pouring rain and jump out of the car. It's Ranger Mike Decker of Petit Jean State Park. When he introduces himself, I think, *Mike Decker, really? The same Mike Decker from the Bill Harley stories I used to hear on the kids' radio show? The Mike Decker that is super cool and popular?* Surely the name is a coincidence, but I let the loose association give me the comfort I need, especially with his capable looking truck and clean-shaven head.

Mike inspects my entire house, inside and out, and we discover the entry point for the lightning. The fire ball found the buried telephone line and turned my phone box into melted plastic and ashes.

"Yep, you got a good jolt there. Looks like it didn't get your electrical, but you're lucky. It could've been a lot worse."

As I begin to consider how lucky I am, I hear the deep growl of diesel engines and know the fire crew has arrived. Down my sinuous, overgrown driveway come two fire trucks and a Ford sedan. Oak limbs snap like firecrackers, and I think, *Well, yeah, the trees did need a little pruning.*

J.R., the chief of the volunteer fire department and coworker at my job, pulls his truck around my little circle drive. Marcus, who I also work with as his supervisor, pulls up behind J.R. in a slightly smaller fire truck. Marcus shines with pride in his full fireman uniform. The yellow suit gleams in the rain, and his helmet shows that he's ready for anything. He approaches me as Marcus, the competent, serious fireman, not Marcus, the intern who does my bidding.

J.R.'s uniform consists of oversized pants that have seen better days and many more fires. The suspenders hold them up over his rain-soaked tank top. Out of the Ford comes a couple. I'm not sure why they are here, especially since the man is wearing camo gear. I introduce myself and ask if he's also on the volunteer fire department. "Yep, I'm Paul Fitch."

Oh no, I think. This is the Paul Fitch whose dog always chases me on my bicycle, and on a particular recent occasion, I accidently ran into Pounder as he was nipping at my ankle. I always meant to stop by his house to let Paul know about the incident and make sure Pounder was okay. He seemed fine at the time, but I was too adrenaline-zingy to stop. In this particular moment surrounded by fire trucks, standing in ankle-deep water, I didn't figure this was the best time to bring up bumping his dog with my tires.

After careful inspection, the volunteer fire crew and Ranger Decker decide that the house is probably okay. "Thank you, thank you, thank you so much for coming here. I'm sorry to bother you with this. Thank you for helping my house," I keep sputtering. "I'm so sorry I don't have anything to offer you. Would you like to come in for some tea?"

"No, ma'am, we're fine. That's what we're here for. We're glad to help."

"Oh, thank you, thank you, thank you."

J.R. walks around to the side of the house, and I wonder if he's decided to stay for a while and admire the view from the cliff. "I'm just trying to see how much room I have to back up my truck. How strong is this cement sidewalk here?"

"Oh, it's pretty good."

Within minutes, the rice paddy habitat is transformed into a mud pit. The Bermuda grass I so loathe is ground down into the subsoil layers. Marcus spins his wheels, creating deep ruts, and as he pulls the truck around, a few more oak branches come down. This time, they are the size of small trees. The cement stepping-stones split like communion wafers.

After peeling off a few of the winter layers, I sit on the front porch steps surrounded by what looks like a small war zone. Sweat continues to pour out of me. The rain has let up a little, and it suddenly occurs to me that I have the perfect excuse for the grey hairstreak that's been developing since I was eighteen years old. I'm so exhausted. I could sleep for a week.

It wasn't part of my plan to move back to the South, and like any intimate relationship, I am slowly learning about give and take in this place, on this land.

On this mountain, in these woods, in this green abundance, the shades and colors of July hold this house in a deep-sea forest world. Layers of water-drop-studded flora crawl and curve up and over all that is present, forming a fishbowl around this home. Tiny blue patches speckled throughout the canopy tell me there is still sky above. The distance creates a mystery and I wonder about the blue yonder. I feel a hunger to move from this enclosed verdant world on the brink to the place where a red-tail hawk cries free in the wind, the World of Vastness stretching beyond this small life, these small desires and worries. For now, I'll stay put and round up some lunch.

Taste and see that God is good.
—JESC

View from Petit Jean Mountain from the cabin after the storm

Breakfast with Gay

We meet for coffee two weeks after her husband died. He was to retire that month. She had spent the last year wondering how they would adjust to his retirement. Now Gay had to adjust to his physical absence from her life. Her own mother has suffered with dementia for four years. During this time, Gay has become mother to her own mother. But just for a brief moment, when her mother hears of Frank's death, she becomes Gay's mother again. "Gay, I know you will really miss, Frank," she said as only a mother could say to her daughter.

We meet again a month later. Gay has just returned from a hiking trip out west. She had planned the trip for some time with her niece and decided to go ahead and go. It was met with many challenges. Forest fires kept them from most of the hiking trails. They decided to go shopping. Gay is not a big shopper. She saw an outfit that was perfect for her, but more expensive than what she usually buys. She gets it but keeps wondering, "Can I afford it now that I have a single income? What would Frank think?" As they leave the shop, Gay's niece points to a sign in the window. "Your husband has called and said you could buy anything you wanted."

We meet again two months later for breakfast. We can begin to laugh about all this, but I know it is still very difficult. As we are ready to leave, our waitress tells us someone has paid for our breakfast. A gentleman comes over and tells Gay, "I so admired your husband and wanted to do something to honor him for his wonderful life. When I saw you this morning, I knew I could start by paying for your breakfast." We look at each other and smile, knowing that instead of absent, Frank is very much present.

Taste and see that God is good.
—JJS

Breakfast with the Osprey

It is a cold windy day at the beach. I sit bundled up under a blanket on a deck overlooking the Gulf of Mexico with my first cup of coffee in hand. The tall tan and green sea oats bend their heads towards the ocean. The wind blows in from the north, driving the waves out to sea so that the turquoise ocean is almost still. No waves hit the shore. A lone fishing boat slowly motors by very near the shore. At the horizon I can barely make out a barge in the distance. An orange and black Monarch butterfly floats by. It may be conserving energy for its unbelievably treacherous flight from the Alabama Gulf Coast to a valley in central Mexico. I stop for a brief second to say a prayer that it will make it. A single osprey flies majestically high overhead, making carefully calculated crashing dives to the sea in search of its breakfast. The intensely bright sunlight shines directly on the water in front of me. The shimmering of the wind on the waves gives the ocean a constant appearance of tiny sparkling lights rising and falling out from the sea. A flock of pelicans float and dive amidst the bright twinkling spectacle. Pairs of dolphins intermittently swim and arch in and out of my field of view. Five Blue Angels soar by in formation overhead as if they are saluting the spectacle below them. As I look out from my balcony I see very few people walking on the beach. It is too cold and windy for Southerners. Alas, a man wearing a wind breaker, gloves, and stocking hat walks out onto the white sand and goes to the surf, but instead of observing the ocean turned into a blanket of shining stars, he pulls out his cell phone and starts talking with his back to the sea. He is missing a once-in-a-lifetime scene. But soon my inner critic reminds me that I have been acting very similarly. Before coming to the balcony, I had spent my morning at a local deli with wifi to check my email. I as well have trouble staying disconnected—disconnecting from the frantic busyness of agendas and tasks to be accomplished and instead reconnecting with the everyday beauty and vastness of a power greater than ourselves.

God help us to *taste and see that God is good.*

—JJS

Breakfast at Kanuga

We are at breakfast at the Bowen conference during Lent at one of our favorite retreat centers, Kanuga, in the western hills of North Carolina. Shortly after we come through the serving line Bea comes to our empty table. Immediately we know this is a special woman. Does Bea mean beautiful? Maybe, but I think the name is short for Beatrice, which means blessed. As we pass to her the famous butter-baked Kanuga toast we learn she is from Beaumont, Texas, but she does not have a Southern accent. She was born in Germany. Her parents were Jewish, but not practicing. She is a Holocaust survivor. She escaped from Germany and lived in Belgium and France where she was helped by the French underground. There she met her future husband, Henry Buller, a Mennonite, who was a conscientious objector doing relief work in unoccupied France and later in England and Germany. She came to this country when she was in her twenties. Is she now seventy or maybe even eighty years old? Actually she tells us she is eighty-four. Bea is articulate and knowledgeable and just an interesting conversationalist. She became a Mennonite but now attends a Disciples of Christ church since there is not a Mennonite congregation in her town, but she says, "I will always be a Mennonite."

We are now joined by Kathryn who comments on Bea's unusual oriental necklace.

"I do not like living alone," Bea says. "It was a gift several years ago from Chinese graduate students who lived with me."

Bea notices my husband's bronze star label pin. She asks how he was awarded it.

"I served in Vietnam," he casually replies.

There is a brief silence. She then responds, "My son, Rene, was killed in the Vietnam War. He was twenty. He was a medic and had only been in Vietnam for two weeks. He was killed trying to care for a wounded soldier. His death was such a waste." Tears fill her eyes. "My son was born on the same day as Prince Charles of England, and whenever I see the prince, I think, this is the age Rene would be. Rene died thirty years ago. He would now be in his fifties, but I can only see him as twenty years old."

We go back to our room in the Kanuga lodge. I have ridden in its slow but steady elevator so many times. Today I see the plaque on the elevator wall. "This elevator given in memory of Reginald Hudson Bedell, RAF bomber pilot, killed in action December 19, 1942. Born

February 13, 1920. Given in memory by his mother, Edna Woods Buist." Reginald was twenty-two. If he were alive today, he would be eighty-five, a year older than Bea. But to Edna Woods Buist and to all of us who ride the elevator at Kanuga to and from our meals, her son, Reginald, will always be twenty-two.

Even in great tragedy we can share a meal and our story and

Taste and see that God is good.
—JJS

Guess Who's Coming to Dinner

Family Secrets

When our three children were young my husband and I were so busy in our medical practice. My husband's mother gave me a book called *Promises to Peter* by Charlie Shedd about raising children. I am so glad I actually read it. There were many suggestions we should have done and never did, but there was one that really worked in our family. One night a week was children's night out. Each week for dinner, one of our children would go with my husband and me to the restaurant of their choosing to have dinner with us. It was our attempt to spend time with just one of our children. I don't know if it was meaningful to them, but it was to us. My husband and I really looked forward to it, except of course when the choice was a greasy fast food place.

Okay, before my daughter tells you, I have a great confession that few know. Here I am writing stories about food, and I stopped cooking dinner in 1982 except for special occasions, Christmas and Easter. For special events I would still cook red beans and rice or sauerbraten. (We called it German roast beef so our children would eat it.) At Christmas I would poach a salmon or bake a rockfish if my father sent us one. We would have a five-course meal with traditional English crackers for Christmas Eve between the children and midnight services at church. Often one of the children would prepare one of the courses: the soup, the fruit, sorbet, the dessert, or the salad. Even though I rarely cooked a meal, I still had a special smell in the kitchen, especially in the winter. I almost always had a pot of apple cider on the stove brewing. It was my most creative cooking, adding a little of this and that for the right taste and smell.

About this time we became friends with another family through our church, and our families began to have Christmas, Easter, and Thanksgiving Day together. We would rotate whose house would host. More people are involved but it is so much easier to share the food preparation with another family. My specialty for Easter was deviled eggs. Barbara always fixed the sweet potatoes and mashed potatoes for Thanksgiving and Christmas. We also shared our extended families and others we knew who would like to be with a big family for the holidays. It often did become a "guess who's coming for dinner occasion."

When I stopped cooking on a regular basis my daughter was six years old. My sons were twelve and ten. My children say they don't remember my cooking except on special events. Why did I do that? I became frustrated coming home from a long day at the hospital, spending much time preparing a meal, and having it all over in fifteen or twenty minutes, at the most. In 1982 I also had surgery on both ankles. I could not walk for six weeks. Friends brought us dinner every night. I just got used not to cooking. We started getting takeout or eating out. All of my children are great cooks, but they learned on their own.

Another confession. My favorite store is Williams Sonoma. I go there several times a month. I don't cook, but I love spending time in a cooking store. What does it all mean? Is this a message from the Holy Spirit that there is a secret unfulfilled part of me that still wants to cook again? I doubt it, for most of the things I buy are cooking utensils for our children and our friends.

Another family secret. When one of our children was a preteen he was expelled from his school for three days. I still remember coming home from a trip and going into our child's room where he was in bed. He got up and gave me a huge hug as I had never had from him before and then went back to bed. I had been at a professional meeting in Boston and been talking to the editor of a medical book about my participation in writing a book. Somehow that hug from my child became a message that there was something not right in our family. I knew from my part that I had been too busy in my work to spend as much time with our family as I should. By God's Grace I took all this as a sign to change myself. I declined writing the book and went to my partners and told them I needed to take a day off from my work. I started taking off Wednesdays. Every Wednesday I was home and I would make brownies. Of course I didn't usually fix dinner, but when my children came home from school, I was there, as were fresh brownies. This was life-changing for me. Whenever I see brownies, I thank God that I was given some insight to be more attentive to my family. I would leave you with my brownie recipe, but as you might suspect, it was always out of a box, usually Duncan Hines.

Taste and see that God is good.
—JJS

Mom's Apple Cider
Apple juice, cinnamon sticks, ground cinnamon, cloves whole and ground, allspice, apple pie spice, ground nutmeg, orange spice to taste. Heat and simmer and occasionally stir.

Mom's Red Beans and Rice
Soak 2 cups of dried red kidney beans overnight in 2 ½ quarts of water. Melt 3 Tbsp. Shortening or bacon fat in an iron pot and sauté 1 large onion chopped and 1 small green pepper chopped. Add the beans, soaking water plus additional water to make 1 ½ quarts with ¼ lb. ham bone, 1 garlic pod, 1 bay leaf, and salt to taste. Simmer slowly for 3 to

4 hours until creamy. Add 2 Tbsp. chopped parsley. Serve over cooked rice. Will serve 6.

Cooking as a Spiritual Practice

My mom stopped cooking in 1982, later saying that it was one of the best decisions she ever made. I have vague memories of her cooking. When I tell people that I mostly grew up eating out at restaurants, I get the you've-got-to-be-kidding-me look. We all have what feels like normal, and this was certainly true for me. It wasn't that I thought all families ate out every night. Dining out was what my family did, and it worked for us. The downside is that I never learned how to cook for myself. Sure, I could open a can of Campbell's soup or make toast, but anything beyond that, and I was stumped.

When I married at 21, I wanted to be a good wife and cook for my husband while he worked nights at a gas cap factory. This resulted in calling the Grant County fire department twice, fighting one small kitchen fire, and suffering through dozens of culinary disasters. I learned that if I stuck to a recipe, I was golden, but even this process was painstaking. Learning how to cook on your own is like learning a foreign language and then attempting to speak a few words. You feel like you have a mouth full of marbles. My husband, on the other hand, had what I thought was a magical gift bestowed upon him. He could make gourmet meals out of nothing without the use of cookbooks or family recipes. I marveled at his ability to intuitively know which ingredients work well together. I felt like this knowledge was far beyond my reach in a distant galaxy. I was attempting brain surgery when my natural gift was singing operatic arias. Chris assured me and told me that his cooking skills developed out of necessity over years of experimentation. I formed a safety net by compiling successes in a black binder and returning to these like a devoted pupil. These were recipes I found in women's magazines at the doctor's office, my grandmother's nursing home cookbook, and a Southern cookbook my mom gave me. Most of the recipes involved deep-frying, rolling balls of ground beef in bread crumbs, or adding lots of pepper to a few limp ingredients. They were simple, unimaginative, fairly unhealthy, and all very doable. I was on the road to cooking fluency.

Sixteen years later and newly married to another man who knows his way around a kitchen, I am now what many would call a foodie. I collect cookbooks as if they're ancient treasure-holding mystical and tantalizing roadmaps for extraordinary gastronomic pleasure. I am one of those people who savors the taste of place. I like to know where my food comes from, support local farmers and markets, and carefully select food based on its story. Three years in a row, I organized an heirloom tomato tasting festival for the nonprofit I was working for in central Arkansas. I couldn't have been happier researching and tracking down gems like Cherokee Purple, Arkansas Traveler, and Mortgage Lifter. More so, it was even more of a treat to visit with the farmers and listen to their stories of life in rural communities.

***

When I was a child, I had a secret hiding place in the woods behind my house. There was a creek, which I later realized was a drainage ditch. For me, the concrete tunnel feeding into it was integrated with the natural landscape, and I never questioned its presence in the forest. In fact, I enjoyed climbing through the tunnel and scrawling pictures with sedimentary rocks on the curved walls. My brothers and I would yell in the tunnel, delighting in our echoes. This place in the woods was also host to an important imaginary world. The world of my making centered on pretending to be a farmer and self-sufficient woodsperson. I had my plot of imaginary vegetables, sturdy tree limbs to serve as farm implements, and rocks for grinding acorns. I collected clay in the creek to make vessels. This world was incredibly fulfilling, and I'm not sure why or how it developed except that I was born with an innate desire to be connected to the land. I think a lot of us are. Some of us are lucky to have special places that are all our own, where we can be whoever we want to be in our imagination.

***

Decades passed before I actually learned how to plant a garden and care for it with a basic understanding of ecology and biodiversity. I've also learned that farming is not well suited for solitary types who think they can do everything themselves. In order to survive, it seems, you have to know your neighbors, have a relatively good relationship with them, and recognize the importance of interdependent connections. I spent several seasons working on an organic farm in New Brunswick, Canada. The days I spent shoveling manure by myself or marking lines for planting in the rain or digging row upon row of parsnip, I would begin to wonder about the fluidity of my sanity. They say that when you sing in church, you pray twice. When you have help in the garden, something similar happens. There is a communal rhythm in our shared efforts. Singing often occurs, lifting the spirit even more to a place where the impossible suddenly feels possible. We will plant the garden this year. We will accept what comes whether it's too much or too little rain, pigweed, or pests. We will harvest thousands of turnips and potatoes. We will share this load together, and we will celebrate and feast together. Sharing in these tasks is a true thanksgiving.

On a few occasions, I smuggled a small pumpkin in my luggage to proudly deliver the fruits of my labor to my family in Arkansas.

Handing the pumpkin over, my eyes were bright with wonder, and nothing could shake my certainty that this was the best gift ever. My parents graciously received the orange vegetable as parents often do with their child's drawing du jour. I puzzled why the pumpkin just sat there on the kitchen table for days instead of being prepared, and then I realized I was expecting my parents to miraculously turn into different people: people who cook at home.

***

While my mom drew a line in the sand with home cooking, there was a special place for baking bread. These memories are vivid, and they include standing in the kitchen with her, or sitting on a stool and kneading the tough mounds of dough. For Easter, we made pretzels from scratch. Laying one arm of dough over the other, my mom explained the shape's symbolism with the cross. We sprinkled rock salt on top of the pretzels and baked them until they were chewy on the inside. My mom recently gave me the scooped wooden bread bowl passed down from her grandmother. I can't help but wonder about the grandmothers I never knew when I look at that bowl. I wonder about its many stories. I feel connected to generations of women in my family each time I use it.

I recently started experimenting with gluten-free baking. I thought it would be nice to offer an alternative to the rice cracker at communion for those parishioners with gluten allergies. Talking on the phone with my mom, I shared my nervousness about baking gluten-free bread. Our choir director told me that the pumpkin buckwheat loaf I made tasted like a packed beaver dam. My mom stopped making bread after the sourdough starter began crawling out of the refrigerator door each time she opened it. She said it looked like it was trying to escape. She assured me about my baking fears and said, "Oh, you know I used to make communion bread all the time for St. Mark's. It was my thing. Do you want my recipe? I can give it to you right now."

"Um, okay. Sure."

"Okay. First, go to the freezer aisle of the grocery store. Then pick up a tube of Pillsbury French bread. Bring it home. Open the tube. Split the dough in half. Shape it into a round loaf. Use a knife to put a little cross on it. Stick it in the oven. Done."

"Seriously?"

"Oh yes. When Steve and Sharon Kemp approached Father Glusman about getting married, they said they wanted homemade communion bread for their wedding. Ted told them they needed to talk to Joanna Seibert because she made the absolute best communion bread."

I'm fairly certain Father Glusman went to his grave not knowing my mom's famous communion bread came out of a can, and this is probably a good thing given the widespread knowledge in the community for his passion for cooking.

We all have fantasy lives. Mine included pretending to be a farmer when I was a child. I never expected to learn how to cook, but it happened through trial and error in what often felt like a glacial pace. My mom's fantasy life involves shopping at her favorite store, Williams Sonoma. For a person who doesn't cook and is a survivor of cooking for young children who inhaled their food within minutes, my mom loves shopping at this store. Loves. They know her by name. This must be some kind of spiritual therapy for her. Williams Sonoma is a shiny, clean culinary wonderland, full of possibilities, possibilities that have been shaped into nonstick Cathedral cake molds, peppermint bark, and gleaming copper cookware. There is every-color-of-the-rainbow Le Creuset pots and pans. You have your choice of not just one artisan salt, but four or five. My mom's primary purchases tend to be holiday treats like hand-painted sugar cookies or chocolate-covered vanilla marshmallows. These are for the grandchildren. Tea towels, soaps, and candles are also a safe bet. To this day, the chestnut candle is my favorite. One of our rituals is checking out the clearance items at Williams Sonoma and then resting with our purchases at the Starbucks next door. Green tea latte for me. Iced decaf Americano with two Sweet n' Lows and no whipped cream for her.

I have no feelings of remorse around my mom's decision to stop cooking. The memories of baking with her are more important than any homemade meals I missed out on. I've been thinking lately that her decision was a natural response to a larger social phenomenon in American culture. The popularity of cooking shows leads me to think cooking has become a spectator sport. We love to watch people create beautiful, delicious meals. Never mind that a ton of planning, organizing, underpaid interns, lighting, shoppers, and designers went into producing the perfect looking kitchen sets. The popularity of stores like Williams Sonoma is a testament for an underlying hunger in American culture. The desire to create culinary masterpieces is obvious. With all of the exciting gadgets and creative kitchen toys now available for purchase and with the plethora of cooking shows, why aren't more people cooking at home? Maybe they are. My guess is that many of us are struggling with what my mom struggled with as a young mother. I think so much of the struggle is with time. Living the Julia Child life requires a radical renovation of one's concept of time. All those fancy gadgets require some forethought and planning. Cooking requires a space of quiet in the soul to wonder about possibilities. Imagination and inspiration grow out this place. How do we structure our lives for this internal place bearing fertility? Shall we take a Buddhist moment and meditate on the vastness of our kitchens, on the life force pulsating, the umbilical cord of generations of humans providing, for better or worse, for the people they share a space with?

Most growth begins with small steps forward. Shall we step forward together and share a meal?

Perhaps we could start with a homemade pretzel.

Taste and see that God is good.
—JESC

Seibert Family Easter Pretzels
1/8 cup hot water
1 package active dry yeast
1 ½ cups warm water
1/3 cup brown sugar
5 cups flour
extra flour
coarse kosher salt
baking soda

Heat oven to 475. In a large bowl, mix the hot water and yeast until the yeast dissolves. Stir in the warm water and the brown sugar. Slowly add 5 cups of flour to the mixture, stirring constantly. Continue stirring until the mixture is smooth and does not stick to the sides of the bowl. Put the dough on a lightly floured board. Dip your hands in the extra flour. Knead the dough until it is stretchy and smooth. Push it down and away from you with the palms of your hands. Turn the dough as you work.

Grease two cookie sheets very well. Sprinkle each with coarse kosher salt. Set the sheets aside. Pinch off a piece of pretzel dough about the size of a golf ball and shape it into a pretzel.

Fill a frying pan with water. For each cup of water in the pan, add 1 tablespoon of baking soda. Bring the water to a gentle boil (a few bubbles). Use a spatula to lower each pretzel into the frying pan. Count very slowly to 30. Then lift the pretzel onto the greased and salted cookie sheet. Repeat until all the dough is used.

Sprinkle kosher salt on top of the pretzels and bake them in the oven for 8 minutes or until the pretzels are golden.

Arkansas

You are there inside me, and it has taken me decades to know your
Bones
Roots
Light
Woven within.
I mistook the ugliness people are capable of for your heart,
And I understand now, this was a mistake.
You are homemade bread shared with Episcopalians.
You are hand-turned bowls holding the dough my mother teaches me to
knead.
You are sedimentary rock layering the creek offering clay.
You are a handmade life, known by the land and expressed through
Wooden colored pencils, hot mulled cider, chilled October sunlight,
and early Church hymns.
Thank you for the scent of oak leaves in the fall.
Thank you for granddaddy long legs and old, worn down mountains.
Thank you for cornbread, collard greens, and thick Southern accents.
You've got my heart.

—JESC

Local Food Dating Leads to God

Black diamond earrings, red lipstick, short leather boots—that's what I've been wearing since I married a priest. Dennis plays Americana songs on his guitar and wears worn-out cowboy boots passed down from the Episcopal Archdeacon in Arkansas. It was Dennis' kiss on the porch across the street from St. Peter's that got me. And then it was through my belly with his good cooking. Chili, gumbo, fish, barbecue— he does it all. One of Dennis' college friends told him that her mother instructed her not to date the boys in Trumann. If I had known boys from his hometown had such big hearts, I would have blazed a trail to the Mississippi River Delta decades ago. I proposed marriage on the third date.

Dennis tells me it was the night I took him to the turkey slaughter that he knew he wanted to marry me. We both had to step back to keep the feathers from landing on us. Or maybe it was the Amish-Mennonite wedding meal we attended earlier in the evening way out in Bellville. The Stutzmans built a fire outside after dinner, and we sat on hay bales beneath a coal black sky. Either activity offered enough evidence that there was something more than good kissing. I hadn't planned on impressing him with such a fine date. It was all luck and having a sheep farmer as a neighbor. I couldn't pass up Ed's invitation for a homemade meal with the Amish-Mennonite family I had been working alongside at the farmer's market.

Or maybe it was the first date that sealed the deal. Dennis invited me to a fancy Italian restaurant in Conway, midway between Little Rock and my home on Petit Jean Mountain. I didn't know it was a date, but his offer of Mike's Place stirred up butterflies in my stomach. Mike's Place is full of romantic ambience with real linen table clothes and individual olive oil dispensers. "How about we go to La Lucha instead?" I asked, "It's in this young couple's home at a busy intersection, they serve local food, and people can make donations in a basket. Oh, and the parking is terrible."

"That sounds like the adventure option," he said, "Let's go for it."

Dennis later told me he looked La Lucha up on the internet, and the only information he could find related to Mexican wrestling. He wasn't entirely sure about what he was agreeing to.

It turned out La Lucha was also the new watering ground for Conway's local chapter of Green Drinks, the social hour for people interested in environmental issues. When Dennis and I walked through the front door, we were greeted by people who all knew me—professional colleagues from my day job at the Rockefeller Institute. They assumed we were there for Green Drinks. Dennis says looking back that it felt like we crashed someone's dinner party. The dining room table was fully occupied, and, frankly, I wasn't there to discuss enlightened topics of that nature. Dennis and I split the single square of lasagna left in the Pyrex pan and hunted down plates and cutlery in the kitchen. Our only seating option was a loveseat in a side room.

Fact: When Dennis kissed me, I was stunned. He parted his mustache, leaned in, and scooped me into an embrace.

"Dennis, I need you to understand something about me."

"Yes," he patiently responded.

"I may have grown up in the Episcopal Church, but I didn't always go to Sunday School. In fact, I'm pretty sure my dad took me to Shipley Donuts most of the time. I have a *natural* spirituality. The church has always been there for me, but I haven't always been there for the church. The point is, I don't know all of my Bible stories, and I'm not sure I really have my colors or chronology straight on the liturgical seasons."

"Joanna," he paused, "Do you think I'm interested in you for your Biblical knowledge?"

Well, I thought, *you are a priest. Don't most priests want to marry Bible scholars?* Boy, was I naïve.

The kiss felt good. Really good. Two parts of me collided. The first shot up guardrails and ticked the reasons why this trajectory could be a mistake. The second raced my heart. At 35, I had paid my dues and knew there was a difference between hormones and connection. Between lust and a deeper undercurrent. The kiss sparked a glimpse into something entirely new.

My next concern lighted on a memory from childhood. I saw dozens of visits with my mom to the Laura Ashley clothing store in the mall. Logic dictated that marrying a priest equaled wearing floral smock dresses. My rational mind knew enough clergy couple examples to deflate the stereotype. But I still saw the buxom priest wife play the organ, bake for charity, organize bazaars, sing perfectly in the choir, hold her own authority over the flock, and wear floral print dresses from Laura Ashley. (I also know spouses who are artists, doctors, professors, lawyers—all strong, independent types—people I would feel lucky to call friend.) Still, what the heck does it mean to fall in love with a priest? Can you cuss and shout the Lord's name during sex? Do you have sex? These matters are never discussed in church. I kissed him back.

"Joanna, I'm getting ready to move to Seattle. I don't want my feelings to worry you. It's not like I'm going to park a VW bus in your driveway and hold vigil. I just needed to get honest with you."

"Thank you, thank you, for being so honest. I'm moved and overwhelmed and cautious, and I feel something too."

"You just need to know that I'm in your corner."

For our third date, Dennis ducked out of the evening portion of clergy conference on Petit Jean, and we drove to Stout's Point.

"You wanna get married?" I asked.

"You wanna marry me?"

"Heck yeah."

***

Dennis and I are married three months later during the Sunday service between the sermon and the peace. I wore a handmade, raw silk dress the color of emeralds and a Japanese-inspired patchwork robe. Dennis wore his favorite tie designed by Gerry Garcia. Our families join us, and we are lifted up and held by our new congregation. Three weeks prior, Dennis was released from Swedish Hospital after five weeks of fighting a staph infection. The doctors do not know why he succumbed to septic shock, but death skirted the edge of his ICU room for weeks. His wedding suit hung on his thinner frame, but I did not notice this until a few months later when I looked at our wedding photos.

My physician parents say it was a miracle that Dennis survived. He recovered from septic shock, but I went into spiritual shock. Before Dennis' near-death experience, I had a knack for carving redemption out of pain, sadness, frustration, and uncertainty. Even in darker times, I had settled comfortably into a spiritual space that said, *All will be well, no matter what. You are strong and full of life.* This message was a chariot through divorce, another failed relationship, and living alone on a mountain's edge in central Arkansas. I felt held and assured. I felt God's support pulsing through all creation. Even the clay and sedimentary rock cleaved to my house as if it were cradled. After Dennis' illness and full recovery, I still knew all of these things, and believed them, but I was left with the question, *So what?*

Joan Didion found security in geology after her husband died suddenly. In what can be known and touched through the movements of rock, water, and wind. Then she found the Episcopal liturgy. Then the beautiful intentionality of creating a home life. Patricia Hampl writes: "Death is central to the usefulness the spirit seeks as its true identity." Dennis didn't die, but something else inside me does. My childhood notion of God.

During the Feast of St. Francis mass I realize my understanding of God carried an unconscious assumption that God would shelter me from terrifying, soul-shaking events just as my parents offered protection in a safe and nurturing home away from the world's evils. That I was somehow special, shielded from the really scary stuff. I even pictured a golden, shimmering armor around my body.

***

Three years have passed since our local November meal at La Lucha. The Mt. Baker neighborhood is now our home in the Pacific Northwest. St. Clement Episcopal Church is part of my family, and I am part of them. I am a clergy spouse. There have been no sightings of Laura Ashley shops in Seattle. My new identity includes making Bloody Mary's at coffee hour, learning the art of Ukrainian Easter eggs, sharing in dozens of home-cooked meals, hiking through rainforests, singing Swedish at a St. Lucy service, and attending my first-ever burlesque version of the Nutcracker. All with parishioners. They're a great bunch.

The gift of living in a rectory means there is a sanctuary in my backyard, and each time I go to church, a small miracle occurs. A spark of insight, a feeling of warmth, a smile, a child's innocence, a sense of the Holy Spirit present in the congregation—something happens, and I leave with a full cup. So, why do I not sing and dance for every opportunity to attend services, to deepen my spiritual practice? Why do I have days where I feel more inclined to lounge on the couch and surf the Internet? I am still trying to understand this new God, a God whose promise I want to believe is for healing. "Sounds like God is messin' with you," Dennis says. In the meantime, Dennis and I create our home with treasures found at thrift and consignment shops. We dance in the living room. We cook gourmet meals. We invite friends over for dinner.

As I go about my days in Seattle, there are moments when I tell myself to remember the words from the Feast of St. Francis mass. I didn't feel like attending mass that Wednesday. I was content reading in the comfort of my den. Dennis called on his cell phone from the sanctuary and asked if I'd be willing to come over. Father Bob, the associate priest, was leading the service. I slipped on my short leather boots and a fleece sweater and ran down the steps of the rectory toward the church. I crossed myself with Holy Water at the baptismal font and walked down the carpeted aisle toward the chancel. Sometimes I can bow at the cross, usually when I know the congregation may be looking at me, and other times, like now, it's harder to bow. I sit down in the pew next to Dennis, and we begin. We pray, read from the New Testament, the Gospel, and then Father Bob delivers the homily. Though I'm sure I've heard these thoughts hundreds of times in sermons, I hear Father Bob's words as if I am entirely un-churched. I hear that people are transformed by prayer. Actually changed. They become new selves. To *become* a new self. I want that. I want the *So What* to disappear. It's quite simple. Gaze upon Christ, consider Christ, contemplate Christ, imitate Christ. These steps become a pathway. If only I can remember them.

After the service, I am haunted by Patricia Hampl's words: "Obedience belongs to necessity, not to a willful search for purpose." She later asserts, through her study of Simone Weil, that our purpose is to consent to the existence of "all that is." How can a person ever truly do that? Maybe there are moments, but to live each day with this acceptance is a tall order. Does *All That Is* include grace and miracles? If so, then maybe. In the meantime, friends are arriving for Sunday dinner. We must prepare.

November Menu for a New Life:
Mac and Cheese made with Beecher's cheddar
Parisian bread from The Essential Baking Company
Yukon gold potatoes roasted with onions and garlic
Spinach salad
Braised kale
Smoked almonds
Hard ginger apple cider
Pandora Radio set to The Avett Brothers

Taste and see that God is good.
—JESC

Wedding Day

Mabel

When I start to beat myself up about not cooking, I remember that one of my grandmothers also did not cook. She always had a large, African-American cook, Mabel. Now I am starting to learn more about my Southern roots. I never knew Mabel's last name even though I saw her almost every day through the twelfth grade of school and more. She lived in a real shanty in a swampy part of town just below my grandparents' house. Of course she walked to my grandparents in all kinds of weather. I remember one time I went to her house with one of my parents to see if she could work an extra day. She had no phone, no lights, no electricity and the road to her house was not paved even though it was a part of town. What I remember most is that I did not think anything was wrong with all this. It was just the way things were. My grandmother also never went to the grocery store. My grandfather had a jewelry store next to the A and P. He did all the grocery shopping at lunch or after work. He would walk home from his store every day carrying the A&P's day-old bread and cakes and milk. They had a garden and chickens so much of their food they raised.

So if not cooking is in my blood, I think it is stopping with me, for my daughter is a great cook, as are my sons. I want to dedicate this story to Mabel and ask her forgiveness for never being aware of how her lifestyle should never have been taken as the way things are. I wish I had paid more attention to how she cooked her greens and beets and green beans and fried chicken and pecan pie. I think one of my cousins did watch her and wrote down some of her recipes. I will try to find them and *taste and see that God is good.*

—JJS

Mabel's Recipe for Rolls
(Also happens to be the same recipe as my Grandmother Johnson's)
1 cake of yeast
2 Tbsp sugar
2 Tbsp melted butter
½ tsp. salt
½ tsp. baking soda
2 cups buttermilk
3 or more cups unbleached flour

Cream yeast and sugar with fork until creamy or liquid. Stir in cooled butter, salt, soda, and milk. Add 1 cup of flour. Stir until smooth. Add 3 more cups of flour until stiff and smooth. (Use a wooden spoon.) Knead until elastic (8 to 10 minutes). Turn into a greased bowl and cover with a clean cloth. Let rise until doubled (2 hours). Punch down and knead. Roll the dough out on a pastry board (flour on the board). Cut with a cookie cutter or glass. Roll over a greased knife. Put in a greased pan and brush with butter. Let rise until doubled. Bake in 375 degree oven for 15 minutes.

The Bartender

If you have a medical connection, you have probably heard of Alfred Blalock. He performed the world's first heart surgery at Johns Hopkins in 1944 on fifteen-month-old Eileen Saxon who was born with a lethal heart defect called blue baby syndrome. But I doubt if anyone also knows the name of Dr. Blalock's African-American laboratory assistant, Vivien Thomas.

At the height of segregation in Nashville, Tennessee, Thomas is taught master carpentry by his father but dreams of becoming a doctor. But in 1930 when the Great Depression wipes out his savings, at age nineteen he takes a low-paying job at Vanderbilt University Medical School as a janitor in Dr. Blalock's lab. But Thomas's carpentry skills soon elevate him to Blalock's trusted laboratory assistant.

When Blalock's growing reputation leads to a position at Hopkins as chief of surgery, he makes it a condition that Thomas accompany him. In 1941, Thomas, his wife, and two young daughters move to Baltimore. In that city and at Johns Hopkins, Thomas encounters prejudice, racism, and segregation as never before. Blalock and Thomas are colleagues and collaborators in the lab, but are never allowed to eat together in the cafeteria. Thomas only enters Hopkins by side entrances and wears a white coat only in designated parts of the hospital.

Inspired by pediatric cardiologist Helen Taussig, Thomas and Blalock spend a year investigating blue baby syndrome and together devise surgery to correct it. As Blalock attends to his many administrative duties, Thomas does the day-to-day work to develop the surgery and creates specialized instruments for the exacting procedure.

In November 1944, the critically ill Eileen Saxon is wheeled into the operating room. With Thomas at his side, directing his every move, Blalock embarks on a desperate attempt to save her life. At Blalock's insistence, Thomas stands on a stepstool just behind him in the OR Thomas has done the operation hundreds of times on laboratory animals. Blalock has performed the entire procedure only once.

After ninety minutes, Blalock begins to sew up Eileen's tiny arteries, no thicker than a matchstick. When the clamps are removed, the baby's blue lips blush a bright pink. Writes Thomas, "You have never seen anything so dramatic. It is a miracle." Alfred Blalock and Vivien Thomas successfully pioneer an operation that brings fame, glory—and hundreds of sick babies to Hopkins. The former carpenter with no college education continues to direct Blalock's research laboratory, and now personally trains the country's brightest young surgeons as well as going to surgery with Blalock. The surgeon holds the scalpel, but Thomas is guiding him through the procedure. Hopkins becomes the most famous department of surgery in the world. Thomas opens new paths for healing for others at a time when all doors have been closed to him.

Yet Thomas struggles to make ends meet and moonlights as a bartender at Blalock's home at parties attended by the same surgical residents he trains during the day.

We only know a little of Thomas's spiritual life, but one episode gives us a clue as to how he survives his cross-bearing.

The first time Thomas performs this life-saving surgery in the laboratory, Blalock examines the incision. He asks, "Are you sure you did this?"

His reply is, "This looks more like something the Lord has made."

Vivien Thomas, a man who lives most of his life as a servant because of his race and the economic times in which he is born, but a man who becomes a leader as he personally saves the lives of thousands of critically ill children and trains hundreds of the world's leading surgeons who still continue to heal today. We first hear about Thomas in the 1960's in Memphis from Earle Wrenn, the pediatric surgeon who trains us and who also was trained by Thomas. Through Vivien Thomas, God transforms a janitorial job into a servant leadership opportunity for healing and teaching, as few others in their lifetime have ever experienced.

Today when I am at parties I try to notice those who are serving and say a prayer for their struggles and their ambitions, knowing they may have other servant ministries.

Taste and see that God is good.
—JJS

Vivien Thomas portrait at Johns Hopkins Hospital

Mealtimes

It seems that mealtimes, whether out in a restaurant or at home, are the only times we are together in our family. Now it seems to be happening less and less as we more often gather around a television watching the horror of the world news tonight as we eat at home or we are too busy with all kinds of night-time activities to get together. There is an amazing bond that can develop for people who share a meal together on a regular basis. All religions know this. When I first became the senior member of our medical practice we were all individuals with very different views and agendas. We started having lunch together once a week and soon our relationship changed. We didn't always talk about work. We learned a little about each other's lives, what was important. We started to work together as a group with a shared vision supporting each other. We learned a little of each other's history.

I live in a family of history buffs. Two of our sons majored in history and my husband's secret passion and bliss is studying and reading ancient history. Our dinner conversations are often a trivial pursuit of the ancient world. I also want my children to know about our own family history I have known or heard about. It seems that mealtimes are the best and now the only time to talk about this. Perhaps this is part of our Jewish heritage. I want our children to know about our ancestors and how they were taken care of just like the Israelites in the desert. I also feel a need to tell our own story. I want them to know about the car accident when I was in medical school one rainy January night in 1967. I had to drop out of school for six months, but the new class I entered is where I met their dad. My life is still limited by handicaps from that accident, but I rarely curse them. I could have been even more impaired. I also have had a realization that I was led from that tragedy into a new life. People in 12-step programs speak of the same experience—the tragedy of their addiction led them to a new life, never realized. The miracle is there, already happening, waiting to happen. That story is the theme throughout the history of our religion We must see it, tell and listen to each other's story—and for some reason, we will forget it if we do not tell it over and over again. Mealtimes have become the best and only time to tell our story and to invite those who came before us to be present again in our stories.

Taste and see that God is good.
—JJS

Liminal Cuisine

lim·i·nal adjective \\'li-mə-nᵊl\\

1: of or relating to a sensory threshold
2: barely perceptible
3: of, relating to, or being an intermediate state, phase, or condition: in-between, transitional

Skirting the Surf: Beginning a Marriage

I knit on the plane—a gray and white pattern of soft wool for my husband-to-be. I picture us wrapped in this blanket made by hand. Circling over Seattle, I see the Space Needle, Puget Sound, the islands, and the downtown cluster of buildings. The land, water, hills, trees, and people seem to join together as a puzzle. I don't know about the havoc of earthquakes or that Pioneer Square was built on sawdust. There is no room in my mind for considering unforeseen instability. All I can see is a mysterious city by ocean water. My eyes widen as the plane circles closer to the landing strip.

***

The first time I visited the ocean was on the Alabama Gulf Coast. I wriggled out of my father's arms and ran toward the water. I had no fear of the waves or the vast expanse of the ocean. Ecstatic delight filled my child body. Each time I am near seawater, there is a primal sense I am home. There are recurring dreams where I am held underwater by the surf. The waves roll me onto the sand continuously. My body is pounded against the coarse grains. Over and over, I am held and thrown by this little womb of water. Eventually, I let go of my need for breath, and realize I can breathe freely underwater. In my letting go, in being carried by this immense power, I am filled with peace. Infinite peace. I am grateful when this dream returns.

***

Walking through the SeaTac Airport, I see Dennis midway on an escalator. At the foot of the stairs, he kneels down on the linoleum and slips a diamond band on my ring finger. It's a Sunday afternoon, and he is still wearing his clerics. "Yes, I will marry you." A thought flits through my mind: *How often do priests propose in airports? Will we get in trouble for our red cheeks? Kissing by the conveyor belt?*

The day after I arrive in Seattle, Dennis wakes feeling queasy and weak. We spend the next three days treating what we think is a stomach bug. By the fourth day, the symptoms worsen, and uneasiness seeps into my own body. I watch with uncertainty while he strains for breath, and excruciating pain runs up and down his legs. When Dennis begins to cry out for the pain to end, I call 911.

The paramedics are remarkably calm. Dennis' blood pressure plummets, and the blue uniformed men act like our long-lost buddies. Dennis is naked, having just crawled from the tub. The paramedics tell us that he needs some form of clothing. All I can find is my flannel pajama bottoms dotted with Russian nesting dolls. They slip them on and strap Dennis to a gurney for the ambulance. Cotton mouth strikes, but we can't give Dennis any fluids. We are like little children in this new city by the ocean after midnight. The wee hours of New Year's Eve.

In his early thirties, the ER doctor has a pierced ear. A tsunami couldn't sway his gelled spiky hair. He is focused on seconds remaining, rather than minutes, to make decisions. I run to the bathroom. When I return, Dennis is vomiting blood. He is too unstable for transfer to the larger hospital. Tests are done rapidly. It is confirmed: renal and respiratory failure. Septic shock. We are taken upstairs where I sign forms for procedures. Dr. Somebody explains the need. "No, we are not married. I am his fiancée." This is enough, and a nurse named Josh puts a tube down his throat and a line in his neck. I begin to tremble and cry as I speak with my parents on the phone. It must be 3 a.m. for them. I blame myself. I remember my mother's words. "That is not God talking." I feel hands on my shoulders. A nurse with long auburn hair strokes my back and offers me juice. She looks like an angel. I can't remember her name.

My mom calls a priest we've known since I was in elementary school in Arkansas. Andrea lives in Bellingham. Her mother, Dean, worked in the Episcopal gift shop at St. Marks on Mississippi Avenue. Every week I walked the mile from The Anthony School to St. Marks for piano and choir lessons. I often arrived early, and Dean took me to the back office for instant soup. I loved feeling the warmth through the Styrofoam cup.

Andrea leaves her two daughters and husband after midnight to make the two-hour drive to Swedish Medical Center on Cherry Hill. When a nurse tells me this is the name of the hospital, I almost don't believe her. Swedish Cherry Hill? That makes no sense. What is this place?

As I wait for Andrea, I hold Dennis' hand. A machine breathes for him, and tubes deliver medicine to his heart. Fluids are pumped into his body to keep his blood vessels from collapsing. He swells and doubles in size. Within days, his skin will begin to weep from the fluid overload. I hold Dennis' hand, and I pray. I pray for God to remove this mysterious illness from his body. To put the illness in me. Let him live, let me die. Nothing can tear me from the room. I find myself entering a kind of meditation. A constant undercurrent of prayer. I can feel my whole body work itself to become prayer for Dennis' wholeness. I am ready to leave this life if it means him living. I am ready to make a deal with God.

Andrea arrives. She teaches me about self-care. She gives me permission to sleep. Brings me yogurt and muffins. We make a quick trip to the rectory for clothing and blankets. I want to bring the blue globe lamp. It was our first purchase together at Metsker Maps in Pike Place. I gather home comforts and begin to settle in on the 2nd floor of the Swedish Cherry Hill ICU. The doctors tell me that Dennis has a MRSA infection. They have no idea how or why.

Raised in the Episcopal Church, I never learned the practice of spoken improvisational prayer. I feel a desperate need to pray aloud, and yet I have no *Book of Common Prayer* with me. I had only just arrived in Seattle a few days before, and a prayer book was not on my packing list. The irony goes deeper when I realize that Dennis is a priest. He lives in a rectory. We are knee deep in books of spiritual significance, but alas, looking for these does not enter my mind as paramedics carry him out the front door. I intuitively pray through my breathing, through my heart, my spirit, but praying aloud, just making up words as I go along, feels like attempting a foreign language I have no familiarity with.

My mom comes to my rescue. Over the phone, in her soft-spoken voice, she recites prayers from the prayer book. I repeat them over Dennis. I recite the words awkwardly as I only catch every other word. Instead of saying, "What? Can you repeat that?" I speak the words I am able to hear, hoping this is enough, that God can hear me, even in broken prayer.

> Healing…holiness…be yours
> Peace…love….surround you
> God…a tent….over your bed
> God…support…holy family…God's spirit
> Amen

My parents fly out and keep vigil with us for a week. Never am I more grateful for their medical knowledge as physicians, but I still see a stunned confusion in their eyes. We take turns sleeping and eating. On Dennis' birthday, my mom wishes him birthday blessings each time his eyes flicker. We say happy birthday dozens of times. I read Garrison Keillor's *Good Poems* aloud. I make hearts out of cardboard Starbuck's sleeves. In his twenties, Dennis earned money by repairing upholstered furniture on site. I use the curved needle still tucked in his wallet to create ornaments for his bed. Mom and I knit. She rubs my back. She peers over the shoulder of X-ray technicians while they check Dennis' heart. Dad introduces me to Pho, which is served weekly in the cafeteria and is the best he's had since Saigon in the '70s.

I begin to feel gratitude. For this room. These beeping machines and medicine. I hang Dennis' lucky shirt over the hospital room window. Each time I see it, I say, "We're gonna get you in that shirt."

I play his favorite music—Bruce Cockburn, The Be Good Tanyas, The Flying Burrito Brothers. There is a constant photographic slideshow on my computer. The nurses and doctors need to see Dennis is more than a patient on life support. The nurses say they do not recognize him with his mustache in the pictures. One of my favorite nurses, Karli, later tells Dennis he looks better without his facial hair and he should consider not having a mustache. Early in our stay, a respiratory therapist asks me how important the mustache is. "Oh my, it's really important," I say, "He hasn't shaved it off for over thirty years. Picture Mark Twain with darker hair."

"Well," says the therapist, "Come over here and look at this X-ray of Dennis' chest. You see the tube here going down his throat? Well, it's not going down correctly and it keeps slipping because of his mustache."

"Shave it off," I say with perfect stoicism.

I leave the room to grab a snack in the cafeteria. When I return, Dennis is mustache free, and my mom hands me a surgical glove sealed in a clear biohazard bag. She tells me that when the nurse pulled out the razor, she exclaimed, "Oh, excuse me, ma'am, this is a really important mustache. My daughter would want to hold onto it. Collect it if you can in this glove, so I can give it to her." I wasn't in the room to see the nurse's expression, so I can only wonder.

***

Another Gulf Coast dream visits often. I am standing at the surf. The water emerald green. I see a dazzling array of seashells through the clear water. I scoop handfuls of perfect conchs, whelks, scallops, moon shells, and sand dollars. My palms are covered in color. I wake filled by abundance.

***

Dennis' phone begins to ding with Happy New Year text messages from friends back home. One message comes from his childhood best friend, Wendel. I have heard a few Wendel stories, but in the newness of a whirlwind courtship, the stories hang abstractly in my mind. I know Wendel is someone special, an iconic pillar of strength and steadiness. He and his two brothers grew up in government subsidized housing in Trumann. Their mom barely kept them fed with her paycheck from McDonald's.

Wendel and I introduce ourselves over the phone. Talking with him feels like slipping on a pair of comfortable shoes. It's easy. I feel like I'm already part of his family. When Wendel says he is ready to get on a plane at a moment's notice, I say Yes to a person I hardly know. My hope is for Dennis to hear a voice from his childhood, for him to know that he is surrounded by people who love him, that he is not alone. Wendel's wife, Janis, gives instructions for what he should do when he sees Dennis. "Stand at the bed, and shout him back, need be."

Wendel arrives at the hospital directly from the airport, hugs me hello, and moves directly to the bedside. He immediately prays aloud unlike anything I have ever witnessed. Wendel and Dennis were raised

66

in the Assembly of God. His prayers sound like poems, and I marvel at his ability to connect with God, to speak freely about healing without having to follow along in a book. I wonder, "A Pentecostal church must be a great place to learn how to pray aloud." I see the tent of prayers twinkling over Dennis' bed.

I accept Wendel's offer to buy me dinner in the cafeteria. Grilled salmon and roasted vegetables. Wendel shakes a sugar packet before emptying it into his iced tea. "Joanna, I don't know how much Dennis has shared with you about how we grew up. You seem like the kind of person who's been surrounded by good people. Dennis was such a good friend. I remember going over to his house during the school lunch hour, and he would make me peanut butter and jelly sandwiches on white bread. That was often the best food I'd eat for the day." He goes on.

"I owe so much to Dennis. I'm here because I want to give back to him. If you need me to be in the room and pray, I'll do that. I'm happy to do that. You also need to know that I'm a doer, and I can do things for the two of you." It doesn't take a minute for me to realize how needed his offer is. "Well, Wendel, do you know how to make bed frames? Dennis had plans to build a bed frame but never got around to it. We just have a mattress on the floor, and I don't think he'll have the strength to build a frame when he recovers, much less lift himself off the floor."

"Joanna, I can do that. I can build you a bed."

Relief and wonder wash over me. I am having dinner with an angel.

The next day, Wendel borrows Dennis' truck to buy building supplies at Lowe's. He spends hours measuring, sawing, and assembling the bed frame. The posts alone are massive pine 4x4s. When Wendel returns to the hospital that evening, sawdust still clings to his pants. In the dim light of monitors, Wendel looks down to where I'm sitting. "Joanna, I got it all built. It's quite something, actually. The blueprint Dennis sketched out was a little hard to understand. You can park a car on this bed. It's about four feet tall, so you'll probably need a step ladder for Dennis to climb up."

"Thank you, Wendel. Thank you so much."

***

Just as sudden as the onset of his illness, Dennis turns a corner after four weeks. A respiratory therapist gently coaches him in his breathing for several hours. The therapist's willingness to commit this amount of time feels like the greatest gift ever given. We are helpless, and a stranger named Ruben guides Dennis into wholeness. The breathing tube is successfully removed. Dennis' first words are "Thank you."

Emerging from sedation and breathing on his own, Dennis enters ICU psychosis, a common occurrence in intensive care. Surreal is a more accurate description. I watch Dennis tell stories in an altered state. In his hushed, raspy voice, he sounds like he is channeling a spirit.

Adhering to a regular sleep schedule feels like a Herculean challenge. Dennis will not cooperate with the night nurse or me until we go along with his instructions. Pointing throughout the room, he directs us as if we are in church. "When I say, 'The Lord be with you,' you say, 'And also with you. Okay?'" When our attempts at rational dialogue fail, the nurse and I both say, "And also with you."

"Good," he says, "That's good." And he falls back to sleep.

On another sleepless night, in the height of his delirium, Dennis proclaims, "Into your hands, Oh Lord, I commend my Spirit." I ask him what this means, and he whispers, "I am ready to let go." My eyes widen, and I feel a surge of energy rising from my gut. "Nope. Sorry, that's not an option. You are not ready, Dennis Campbell. You are surrounded by people who love you. You have so much more to do in this world. You offer so much. It is not time to let go." With these words, he falls asleep and awakens the next day renewed. The delirium is gone. Suddenly, his baby steps turn to giant leaps. My first question to the doctor: "Is it okay if we kiss?"

The last week in the hospital feels like a honeymoon. There is the lost time we are trying to make up for. We cuddle in the high-tech hospital bed. We watch movies. Eat popcorn. Picnics in the bed. Talk for hours. We look at the letters and prayers people have posted on the Internet. The nurses try to give us privacy. We kiss. My laughter can be heard down the hallway. I sneak a contraband cheeseburger into the room for Dennis to enjoy while I eat his nutritionist-sanctioned salmon filet. We share French fries and lick the salt and grease off our fingers. We are whole. We are complete. We are whole and complete in our brokenness.

***

On our two-year anniversary, Dennis and I drive to Moclips, Washington, to celebrate in a cottage on the beach. We arrive just after sunset. My first sound is frogs chirping from a shrub-filled gulley leading to dunes, giving way to yards of hard peppery sand stretching on to the Pacific. Water shapes the land, but it's easy to witness this marriage closely on the sand. Spring water rivulets sculpt little worlds across the beach. I see spirals, spinal columns, and fingerprints left by the wind. I count at least ten rows of waves crashing before they reach the surf. Wind blows the cresting water westward. The first half-mile of water must be white foam. Immense. High and low tide are new phenomena to learn.

I forget to do morning prayer on our anniversary. Dennis says not to worry. "We'll do noonday prayer." We forget to do that too. I think of going for a run on the beach. Instead, I eat Boudin for lunch and then for dinner. On the second glass of wine, I say, "We forgot to pray today." Dennis smiles and says, "Not to worry. Today is a feast day."

I walk in the morning. I sing hymns I can't remember the names of but know the words. I improvise soothing melodies, not worrying about who can overhear. As I sing, my eyes scan the surf, and I am caught by a vision. Dozens of sand dollars peek from the surf. Whole, intact, the size of tea saucers. I gather handfuls. I find rocks bore through by a clam who creates a perfect hole in its turning. Waves absentmindedly leave kelp on the beach. Crab shells punctuate the sand with their purple, red, and orange bodies. Sometimes I see only the claws. Upturned razor clams show their pearly interior world. Dozens of sandpipers fearlessly skirt the surf. They have incredible faith. On several occasions, I catch a glimpse of the approaching tide just in time to move.

Taste and see that God is good.
—JESC

Full Recovery

Sandpipers at the Edge

Morning meditation

How do you piece life together
with the wind knocked out of you?
Follow a thread, an idea to *create*—
a poem, a batik…hopefully a story.
Even if you don't believe—
live as if you do.
Each day, there is a little more breathing.

Feel the cool salt air in the morning.
Warm yourself with the coffee
made by your husband
who is *alive*
by prayer, miracle, and medicine.

I know what the other side of longing feels like.

God has my attention.

—JESC

Tasting the Present:
What I Have Learned from My Daughter

I have learned the most about tasting, living in the present, from my daughter. Of course, she tells me she learned it from her husband. However, I remember when she was a little girl when she ran into our kitchen screaming out as best she could, "Mommie, come out, come out, and see the rainbow." By some miracle, I stopped my agenda and went with her to our front yard where the sprinklers were watering our lawn and there were a myriad of rainbows in the mist. Twenty years later, my husband and I spent a week at the beach with our daughter. As the sun was setting we had a picnic on the beach and were taking those famous dusk beach pictures dressed in our best white. Just as we clicked our last picture, a spectacular rainbow appeared in the pink clouds just in front of us over the blue waters of the Gulf. We were out of film. I ran into the house searching for any film I might have forgotten I had. My family called out, "You're missing it." Alas, I returned and stayed with them as the rainbow faded and then reappeared and the pink clouds moved in and out the spectacular prism, all orchestrated by the sun setting in the opposite horizon. We could only soak in that gift of nature for a brief time in space and hope we could capture that once-in-a-lifetime Kodak moment in our memories.

My daughter talks to me about her sitting for long periods of time on the shore watching a blue heron at the water's edge doing the same, patiently waiting for its dinner. And so today I sit by the sea and wait for the rainbow and wait for the blue heron, and hope that they are also still waiting for me.

Taste and see that God is good.
—JJS

Wood Smoked

As I guide the imperfect wood into the press, I wonder if a sawyer at Plum Creek gets close enough to the wood to see the variations, the little universes. I've been working at RBM Lumber in Columbia Falls, Montana, for five days, and I've made an amazing discovery. I'm in love with grade 2 and 3 lumber. I am in love with worm holes, embedded bullets, and rot. Each piece of wood is a feast for my eyes and hands. Swirling stages of decay give value to this lumber. I must resist pausing for too long in my admiration. I keep thinking, "It can't get any better. Surely I've seen it all now." But, no. Every board is a new painting, a new universe. I am held captive by this beauty.

What would be discarded and burned in a larger, industrial mill becomes the specialty product at RBM Lumber. In the woods, owners Ben and Malcolm see a fir that a larger mill would cut without hesitation. They see this tree growing for another fifty years. The rings multiply. It lives that much longer to support habitat, even old growth, they say. Where one mill sees garbage, another sees opportunity, creativity, and, best of all, beauty. There's a chance to see the forest and not just board feet for the short-term.

I am overcome with gratitude for working for a family-owned and operated value-added sawmill. Father and sons. Mother and sons. I live with the M part of RBM Lumber. That stands for Roy Ben and Mom. It used to be Roy Ben and Malcolm, but Malcolm unofficially retired in his early seventies. His contribution anymore is spending weeks at a time living and working in the woods, felling trees, and bringing them to the mill. Mom, or Evelyn, is still the head sawyer after all these years. She's been gracious enough to let me live in the basement apartment of her log home. I just have a few suitcases I'm living out of, and it's enough of a world for the time being.

I tell my friend, Philip, that it's a bit different up here. He says, "Well, it's a small logging town, if that's what you mean." That's not exactly what I mean.

After work, Evelyn invites me up to her living room. She instructs me to bring two beers of my choice. A Red Stripe for her and a Corona for me. She tells me about losing her dad when she was a kid. Her seventeen-year senior brother died in the war. She and her mom and her other brother moved from Colorado to San Diego, where she worked in a defense plant. She hated it, and when her mom died when she was sixteen, she convinced her brother to buy a chicken ranch in eastern

San Diego near the Mexico border. "A lot of desert and heat," she says. But she loved it. They had two hundred chickens and she often had to squeeze them to get the eggs out, and she milked cows in the morning before going to school. That's where she met Malcolm, who was in Future Farmers of America. She said it wasn't love at first sight, but they bonded over their shared interest in agriculture and farming. Married at eighteen, having known each other a year, they started a family two years later, having four kids in five years. After thirty plus years, they decided they were better as friends, and Malcolm decided he was happiest living in a little shack forty yards away.

***

Seasoned cast iron, root vegetables, and wood smoke—these are the smells in Malcolm's home. A chair, pots and pans, folding knife and a forest of life's possessions. Malcolm lives on a sliver of land, surrounded by a carpet of copper needles. Trees, tracks, train, and bluff. A silver dish rack rests in the shade of a Western Larch, and glass jars glisten with morning rain. River, canyon, blinking light, and eagle. This is a wild Thoreau didn't write about.

***

Evelyn encourages me to use her hot tub and offers me fresh baked heirloom squash. My sawmill worn body devours it in one breath.

I crawl into bed around 9:00 p.m. and turn out the light. Soon after, I notice orange light flickering behind my window shade. Malcolm has started a fire on the bluff where he often sleeps. As if getting a telephone call, I immediately throw on some warm clothes, grab a blanket, and wander through the garden to his light. He's brewing hot water in a cast iron tea kettle and offers me a cup. I tell him I once learned when a person is drinking tea with other people, they should never pour their own. Each person should pour for the other. Malcolm tells me about a book he's reading, *Shadow Mountain*, about wolves and how much he relates to the message the author relays: wild animals don't like to be constrained.

Malcolm doesn't want to contribute to the landfill, so what he can't burn, recycle, compost, or reuse, he sprinkles around the shack he inhabits. Evelyn says she gets to a point when she can't stand it anymore and cleans up his place. He tells me about Amigo, Evelyn's dog, who was recently killed by a car. Amigo came to her as a deeply abused animal. He was leery of male people in particular, and never got very close to anyone. Malcolm says he felt like he was a twin to Amigo.

In the morning, I grade 2, 3, Worm Hole, Select, White wood, Vertical, Vertical 2, Circle 2, Circle Select, and Circle 3. As each piece comes through the trimmer, I speak the grade out loud to convince myself of its correct category. Then there are the lengths. Each grade has anywhere between 2 and 10 lengths to consider. At one point, I dance around the stacks like a sandhill crane, shouting the grade and length I am looking for. Perhaps I am in a mating ritual with the lumber; I can't say for sure in this altered state. Thank goodness Dale and Sarah can't hear me. Dale eventually comes over, smiles, and says, "You look lost." His patience is a godsend. I continue in my fight against holding the wood longer than a few seconds; it's a privilege to work with such beauty. By the end of the shift, I am zingy from the intensity—the dizzying grades I must name, placing them quickly in the stacks, feasting on their wild swirling cracked worm-eaten rotting blue-stained world.

Later in the lumberyard I see Malcolm sorting through discarded wood trimmings. He wears a piece of wood threaded on a strand of yellowed cord. I tell him that I like his necklace and ask him if it has a story. He tells me that he wears it precisely so people will ask him to tell its story. He hands it to me and says, "You know what kind of wood it is." Tight rings, small and round. I ask if it's a knot. "Yes," he says, "It's the strongest part of the tree. At least that's what I believe." Durable. Knots are a metaphor for our relationship with the Divine. Quoting the Bible, Malcolm says, "I am the vine, and you are the branches." Jesus is the knot holding us together. In lumber, black knots mean the part of the tree that was dead when it was cut. Blonde knots show the living connections. The connection isn't always clear—the line between life and death isn't obvious. Death is a symbol of the unknown. The veil is thin.

Light morning rains have dampened the fir branches Malcolm gathers later for another fire. Color still lingers over the western horizon. My contribution to Malcolm's offer of burger and tea is sauerkraut, avocado, garlic, bread, beer, and poetry. I tell him we must be communicating with someone, somewhere with the smoke we're sending up. We find dryer wood under a plastic sheet. Evening winds blow the smoke around our bodies. I read *Love Poems from God* aloud—Hafiz, St. Thomas Aquinas, Catherine of Siena. My light is the blaze of Ponderosa needles. Our table is a slab of wood. We slather our fire-cooked burgers with every condiment available and split my last Fat Tire beer. It doesn't take much, we both state, to feel a beer. The smoke has taken its toll, and the quiet of our eating is accented with sniffling and tears spilling down our cheeks. I tell Malcolm I can't think of a better way to have a meal than to cook it on a bluff overlooking the river with the year's most beautiful sunset and a mouthful of spice and tears. "Yes," he says.

In Native American spirituality, a mistake is often intentionally woven into weavings to create an opening for the Spirit to move through. I can't help but wonder if all of the earth-worn types, the black knots, and these decaying jade and powder blue fungi-swirled, worm-eaten boards are other kinds of divine mistakes brought here as some kind of reminder. I can only hope.

Later in the night, I fall asleep under a pile of blankets and stars, pungent garlic still in my mouth and a swirl of wood-smoked hair around my face.

Taste and see that God is good.
—JESC

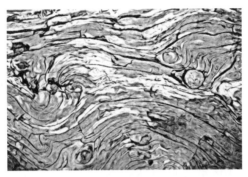

Cracked and Earthworn

Malcolm and Ben

Wood Stained/Kanuga Toast

We arrive early in the morning at one of our favorite retreats, the Kanuga conference center just outside of Ashville. The quiet woods and lake calm my soul as I sit in a large rocking chair on the back porch of the conference center waiting for Morning Prayer and breakfast. I fantasize about our first meal at Kanuga. The food is wholesome but the highlight of dining, especially at breakfast, is the Kanuga toast. The toast is baked hard with butter on both sides. It is as hard as a rock or wood. Some have described it as a giant crouton. It is not healthy, but so delicious, but if you are not careful, you might break a tooth on it. Yoriko Russell from Kanuga describes the twenty-four hour making of this delicacy as an age-old British method of making toast.

Before we partake of our Kanuga toast we walk the short distance to Morning Prayer at the Chapel of Transfiguration just across the parking lot from the dining hall. As we say the Venite, I look at the chapel's wood. I have been in this holy chapel so many times before, but in the morning light I notice for the first time unusual markings on the wood, more prominent in the ceiling. I forget about Kanuga toast and lose my place in the service and wonder what these oval dark markings possibly could be. Is this some kind of special wood?

The leader of Morning Prayer also must have had a similar experience at some time in the chapel, for after the gospel she gives a short homily about the chapel wood markings. She talks about how this wooden chapel, like none other, is built in 1936 of Carolina white pine from trees taken down in an ice storm that year. The chapel is built shortly after the storm and the wood is not pretreated. Now over three quarters of a century later as we look at the walls and especially up at the ceiling we see strange oval and oblong marks that are more prominent and numerous at the highest part of the ceiling. Examining closer we see that these are fingerprints embedded in the wood from the oil of the hands of the carpenters who built the sacred space. The chapel is not insulated so supposedly the cold and heat stained these marks even more prominently and permanently. The number of fingerprints on each board reveals which pieces of lumber are the hardest to install. The fingerprints are like an antique archive of how easy and how difficult the chapel is to construct.

The leader of Morning Prayer goes on to talk about how in a visit our mother or father or grandmother or grandfather we may see their fingerprints on the walls and throughout their homes. Sometimes their fingerprints are in a smell, a picture, a story we remember, a food we remember that was their specialty, a quiet time we had at the kitchen table with them. As we look at any building, church, or home, we will find the fingerprints now invisible of the people who built and sustained these places. We may not see them, but these fingerprints are there, and we as well are called to leave our fingerprints for our children and grandchildren. Our prayers are that we leave more fingerprints holding up those we love as we see these special workers left for us in at the Kanuga chapel.

We return to the service, say the creed, the prayers, and thanksgiving. I say thanksgiving for so many who left their invisible fingerprints of love in my life. I pray that I may do the same and carry on the love they showed to me. The bugle sounds. It is time for breakfast. I can't wait to share this story and Kanuga toast with old and new friends.

Taste and see that God is good.
—JJS

Recipe for Kanuga Toast
Lay white and wheat breads on sheet pans.
Lightly brush each piece with a warm margarine mixture.
Place sheet pan out in a speed rack and zip shut until next morning.
Place bread in the morning in a 500 degree preheated oven for very slow baking (20 to 25 minutes) until the bread has toasted to its famously firm, crispy state.

Kanuga toast

Kanuga Chapel of Transfiguration

Fingerprints on the wood

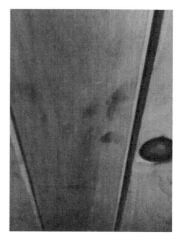

Kanuga ceiling

How to learn how to turn your life and your will over to the care of God:

1.   *Have children.*
2.   *Grow old.*
3.   *Invest in beach property during hurricane season or before an oil spill.*

—JJS

The Big Spill

It is mid-August, 2010, still the height of the summer tourist season on the Alabama Gulf Coast. We arrive at the condominium that has been our family's vacation home for twenty-five years. We are alarmed to see that ours is the only car in the parking lot. Beyond our balcony on the fourth floor, the blue green Gulf is calm, and a cool breeze blows to the east, but only a few isolated sunbathers lie under their umbrellas on the white sandy beaches. Double red flags are flying. No bathers are swimming *in* the Gulf. At dusk arrive a covey of beach buggies called UTVs motoring up and down the beach followed by shiny green tractors pulling covered trailers with benches on either side for beach cleanup workers wearing colored shirts. The color of their shirts is like a liturgical vestment, dalmatic or chasuble, signifying the duty of the worker. The UTVs and John Deere tractors and trailers carry ice chests, portable tents and lights, and Port-A-Potties. They go up and down, up and down the beach, but none stop. Finally one UTV stops near our condominium. Two workers get out and look at the sand near the surf. A half hour later a new John Deere tractor slowly pulls a trailer with workers to the site. They set up a blue tent and folding chairs. The workers sift the sand for twenty minutes and then rest in the folding chairs under the tent. This process goes on all day and night, but seems busiest in the early morning, at dusk, and at night. Next comes a lone person walking slowly like a verger or crucifer in a religious procession striding in front of a UTV followed by a green tractor pulling a large machine that rakes the sand. At night the tractor pulling the sand-sifting machine has two large lights on either side like processional torches. The processional leader is trained to look for alternating or simultaneous right and left flipper turtle tracks in the sand leading to a loggerhead sea turtle nest that should not be disturbed by the mechanical beach rake. My husband goes down to get a closer look at the sand after the parade passes by. He still finds tar balls, especially on seaweed and shells near the shoreline. We see few pelicans, no Great Blue Herons, no dolphins. Only the laughing gulls seem to be unchanged in numbers and squawking. Most noticeably there are no fishing boats leaving the pass to venture into the Gulf for the catch of the day. There is a large permanent boom across the pass and a smaller more portable one around Perdido Island and Robinson Island, two small islands just inside the pass. Hidden under the Perdido Pass Bridge are large white tents as you might see at a revival or the circus. The area is chained off with a guard at the entrance.

At a local restaurant we have no difficulty finding our favorite seat. Sometimes for a while we are the only ones there. We talk to the locals about how they are doing. Most report their businesses falling off thirty to sixty percent. One restaurant has a sign on the door that they no longer can afford to serve breakfast, only lunch and dinner. Another has stopped serving lunch, only dinner. The worst hit are the commercial and charter fishermen and shrimpers. They have completely lost their business. From the window of one of our favorite restaurants by a marina we watch charter fishermen hosing down their boats like boys on a Saturday afternoon washing their cars in expectation for that Saturday night date. For the fishermen the date does not materialize. Members of our family grieve especially for one charter boat captain who frequently took them out to fish. He has committed suicide. A newly established local restaurant and a local seafood market have closed before we can try them out. Henry's, the local furniture store we frequent is going out of business. Only Henry is there answering the phone, showing off the little stock left, and taking last minute orders.

Nearly 185 million gallons of oil have violated the Gulf since the explosion on the oilrig on April 20th of this year (2010) that also killed eleven workers. In the twenty-five years we have been part of the community of the Gulf Coast, we have survived with them minor and major hurricanes such as Frederick, Ivan, and Katrina. This disaster, however, has so many more unknown and long-reaching effects.

Small tar balls in the sand next to a penny

A month later the oil well is permanently capped. We return to Paradise Island, as the locals call it. The parking lot is now three quarters full. We sit on our balcony watching the early dawn turn light then pink then orange. At daybreak three men and three children come to the surf and cast their lines for early morning breakfast. They are simultaneously joined by three, now five Great Blue Herons stalking behind them, craning their long necks as each observes every movement of the fishing lines hoping for a free meal. I cannot hold back tears as we watch small and large fishing boats leave the pass in the early morning to go to unknown parts of the Gulf for more hidden treasures of the sea. A single red flag is flying, but there are now many bathers venturing in and out of the surf at the water's edge. My husband only finds two small tar balls on his morning walk. No workers patrol the beaches during the day. Their guarded headquarters under the Perdido Pass Bridge is still there but is almost deserted.

Flocks of pelicans fly by. Dolphins glide by in parade and occasionally jump for joy. We do not go early enough to our favorite restaurant to get that special table overlooking the marina. Life seems to be restored. It looks like resurrection.

We go in the afternoon to a Eucharist and healing service at a local church to give thanksgiving. People come to the altar rail for healing. As members of the congregation, their priest, and I place our hands on them, they pray through their tears for strength to meet the financial and personal losses they have endured. During the Eucharist we hear a dog constantly barking. At the peace a member of the congregation goes out to find a gray dog with matted hair in its kennel abandoned at the church door. The priest, Chris, interrupts the service and goes out to give the dog water. Another parishioner plans to take the dog to a friend who "needs a dog." Someone could no longer care for a special member of the family so left it with another family they hoped would care. Later at the vet's the parishioner finds out the dog now named Rags is a purebred Lhaso Apso, probably a year old. This breed originated in Tibet and was bred primarily as interior guard dogs for Buddhist monasteries and palaces. It was thought that the souls of the lamas entered the Lhaso Apso while awaiting reincarnation.

We see scars that will be with this community for years to come, but we learn a great deal about what a house of God can be: a place for people in great distress to go for healing in community, to share their pain and be surrounded and touched by the many hands of God.

Back at our condo we read in the paper that a federal survey of the Florida, Alabama, and Mississippi coast finds tar balls still washing ashore with every wave and bands of oil buried under 4 or 5 inches of clean sand in 3 feet of water off the shoreline of nearby Bon Secour National Wildlife Refuge. Other researches from the University of Georgia find oil at least two inches thick a mile below the surface of the Gulf over a layer of dead shrimp and other small animals at least eighty miles from the site of the blowout. My husband walks again on the beach looking more closely and now sees thousands of tiny pea-sized tar balls disguised in the sand. The Old Bay Steamer in downtown Fairhope, a favorite seafood restaurant for twenty-five years, is closing Sunday. The owner reports that sales have bottomed out as people fear eating contaminated local seafood, especially the royal red shrimp, their specialty. Our hearts ache. We look out from our balcony for some hope.

As the bewitching hour of five o'clock approaches, nine cars pull off on the highway shoulder by our condo. Twenty people dressed in black emerge from the cars and go to the beach. There is an apparent leader, a photographer. The dress code for beach portraits must have changed from white to black. We watch for almost two hours as the family gathers in various groups for candid shots. The sandbar in front of our condo has washed away and consequently we have lost much beach. The crashing waves have carved out a shelf near the water's edge with a three foot drop off. The photographer uses the shelf for the family to sit on in various groupings. The shelf has made it more difficult to walk to the surf but how marvelous that the photographer finds a use for it. Farther down the beach we now see a trellis covered with flowers. Four bridesmaids in red dresses arrive with the bride and groom barefoot under their white wedding garments. An ancient liturgy has returned to the beach.

At dusk three people with lime green shirts walk out to a roped-off area about fifty yards from our condo. They have a shovel, a bucket, a stethoscope, and surgical gloves. My husband goes down along with about a half dozen children on the beach to see what this "medical" team is doing. The "green" team demands that all be perfectly still. Perfectly still. A young woman with the green shirt lies on the beach and puts the stethoscope to the sand. She hears movement. They remove the wire mesh previously placed over the Loggerhead sea turtle nest to protect it from coyotes and raccoons. They gently dig into the sand with their surgical gloves, careful not to rotate and move the remaining eggs in the nest and find six newly hatched baby loggerhead turtles that have just absorbed their yolk sac. Demeter herself could not have been more motherly lifting the two-and-one-half inch turtles to the bucket and transporting them to the shoreline. The leader in the green shirt makes a trough in the sand to the surf. The sea turtles are placed in the trench and the crowd cheers as they ceremoniously parade awkwardly to the sea. Loggerhead turtles have been nesting on beaches all over the world for over 150 million years. It takes twenty-five to thirty years for loggerheads to reach sexual maturity. Only one in one thousand, to one in ten thousand loggerhead eggs reach adulthood. Will these six by chance be in this number?

What will be the future for our Gulf? But it is not *our* Gulf. We have been stewards of it now for twenty-five years. It will soon belong to our children and grandchildren. Our hope lies in today's children being photographed with their families, the young couple being married on the beach tonight, the four groomsmen and bridesmaids, the three young people fishing on the surf in the early morning, and in the half-dozen children who cheered the loggerhead sea turtles into the surf this magical night.

We are counting on them to help us.

Taste and see that God is good.
—JJS

The Big Spill a Year Later

We come to the beach to escape from a crisis tearing apart our church. The school associated with our church for fifty-four years that many have so loved has suddenly been closed. We are like the Israelites escaping from Egypt, except it took us two days to get to the Promised Land while it took them forty years. Like Psyche in Greek mythology at the start of each of her tasks to regain Eros' love, and more recently Victorian women of two centuries ago under stress, we fall as gracefully as possible on our couch just designed for fainting. Our fainting couch is the seashore. The waves, the sun, the sand, the quiet, the sunsets, the vastness of the sea—like the antiquated smelling salts remedy, help us at least intermittently to become a non-anxious presence. There are small children playing at the water's edge making sandcastles that will soon be gone in a few hours. Six Blue Angels fly overhead. People on the beach clap with pride as they look up and see the planes in precision formation. The Angels as well have recently had a near-disaster. Fishermen come out in the early morning and cast lines into the blue green surf hoping for a breakfast treat. It has been a little over a year since the big oil spill. It is the first day of fishing season for red snapper. I have never seen so many large and small boats leave their safe harbor at Perdido Pass to venture out just after dawn to catch this succulent food from the sea. We are told that red snapper are abundant since there was no fishing last year because of the oil spill. The oil spill. Another disaster, but this one *here* at the Promised Land. Patrols still comb the beach for tar balls, but we see only one in a week. The people have returned to the beach. Restaurants and businesses are booming. It is hard to rent a condo or house for this summer. Everything is filled up. The sea and the land are telling us that we will survive this. They did. We remember Hurricane Ivan seven years ago. I remember we came to the condo building and could not recognize it, could not figure how to get in. The first floor was washing away. The elevator had been destroyed. It was even harder to *find* the building. There were no street markers or signs. Part of the highway was gone. When we finally found the stairs and climbed the four flights up to our condo, we opened the door to the smell of rotting food in the refrigerator and found the condo blown apart. Then a year later there was Katrina, just as we had almost recovered from Ivan. But the land, the sea, the sand survived. They are telling us *we* can survive as well. There may be scars. I still see trees that are dead and have never had regrowth after the hurricanes six and seven years ago. I only saw one dolphin this week and hear of at least fifty who have washed up on the beach dead. Our wounds will heal, and there will be scars. But like the waves and the sand and the dolphins and the pelicans we will become wounded healers, remembering that there is much pain in the world, as we have tasted from it as well. We know a little about it—we have come through it in the past, and will this time as well by remembering how we were cared for in our past. We know a little more about what to do and say to others in crisis. We will treasure the good times. Things we used to take for granted now become more sacred. We go out to eat for lunch and have fresh red snapper just caught this morning. This time we appreciate it, give thanks for it, and say blessing over it. It has become Eucharist, a thank offering, a sign of resurrection from the sea. Delicious. Delicious!

Taste and see that God is good.
—JJS

Rainbow on the Gulf

Gulfshores
Three and a Half Years Later
Ordinary Day

Someone's rainbow beach umbrella has blown away and is caught in the sea oats on a sand dune,
our daughter swims with a hammerhead shark, and
I walk in the early morning in a cool blue pool.
A turtle nest protected by black plastic waits expectantly in front of our condo.
Dolphins playfully jump out of the water just a stone's throw away as
pelicans and seagulls and blue herons have a feast frenzy on sheets of schools of fish near the shoreline.
We dine on fresh-grilled soft shell crabs.
People of adventure are parasailing as
a rainbow is born in the early afternoon and
the ocean waves grow six feet high.
Our daughter rides the waves, then
brings back gifts from the sea.
I watch her walk tall on the sand into and out of the waves, and then
she sits looking out into the ocean with that reflection of wonder that I first saw when she was a little girl.
Three Blue Angels loudly announce their arrival as they fly by and leave their signature white trail.
We dine on fresh clams in Manhattan chowder,
the moon is almost full and lightens the night.
Fast fluttering bats keep us insect free.
We go to sleep by the rhythm of the waves that are
almost nonexistent, and the sea is now like a big lake as
turtle people come again in the dark.
It must be close to hatching time,
an ordinary day.

—JJS

Cocktail Harp

I have played the harp now for many years and have learned much more from the instrument than just about where the strings live and how to pluck them. Actually I owe all of this to my daughter, also named Joanna. When she was in grammar school she liked this 7UP commercial with a man playing and dancing with the harp. She kept talking about harp lessons. We gave her the usual answer parents say when your children ask for something that you think is just a fad: "We'll think about it. Let's talk about it next week." After a year of her begging, we decided, "Well let's give it a try. Maybe she really means it and is serious about it." As you might expect, harps are expensive and are not sold in the music stores in Little Rock, so I decided because of the expense and because I had heard our daughter talk so much about it that maybe both of us would try to learn to play. After some research, we contacted a harp company in Chicago, Lyon and Healy. Should we get a pedal harp or nonpedal? You move the pedals with your feet to make the strings sharp or flat. Should we get a new one or a used one? We decided on a nonpedal harp with levers that shorten the strings to make the strings sharp. Playing pieces in flats means some maneuvering. Lyon and Healy would ship us their largest used nonpedal harp called a Troubadour to rent. If we liked it, we could later buy it. Sounds like a good deal. Rent to buy. I remember the day when the harp arrived in its huge cardboard case. It was like Christmas. You might think that finding a good harp teacher in Little Rock would be difficult, but not true. I easily found a patient, kind teacher Martha Rosenbaum who actually came to our house and taught both my daughter and myself. One advantage of playing the harp is that your teacher will come to you. Of course, the disadvantage is when you go anywhere with the harp, you will need some major help, like my patient husband who has become the harp bearer.

Well, what do you think? After a couple of years, our daughter decided not to continue her lessons, but in my heart, I know she will take it back up at another time. I, on the other hand, got addicted to it and couldn't stop.

I play now mostly at my church and at retreats and do occasional weddings and special events for friends. The special events I call "cocktail harp." I play while people are dressed up in their finery, drinking cocktails and eating light or heavy hors d'oeuvres and speaking pleasantries as they try to maneuver a small plate, napkin, and a glass of wine. I soon realized that no one ever really hears the harp. It is so noisy, but people seem to like the background and the visual appearance of the harp even though they can't really hear the music. At first this was frustrating. I purchased an amplifier for special events so people could hear the softness of the harp. The music still was not well heard over the din of the crowd, especially after many people had had several glasses of wine or beer or champagne. Then I finally decided just to enjoy being there and stop worrying about whether people heard what I was playing. I would imagine that I was subliminally sending calming vibrations into a crowd that was longing for peacefulness. I imagine that I am David playing for King Saul. So far no one has thrown a spear at me. I doubt if I have really calmed anyone else's soul, but this imagery has calmed my soul. I also realized that playing for people who are concentrating on talking and eating and drinking was also a great time to practice pieces I was still working on that were not yet ready "for prime time." I could practice difficult pieces in a crowd and gain confidence that I could play them in front of other people. Sometimes I was embarrassed to take money from anyone for doing these events. So the harp has taught me to adjust to a new situation, learn from it, and go with the flow, especially playing "cocktail harp." It has been my closest experience to "letting go and let God."

If you have any friends who play guitar then you will know they eventually don't have just one guitar but soon have several, sometimes many. Well that is also true of harpists. My husband got tired of lugging this huge harp around, called Lyon and Healy and found out about a smaller harp, a Celtic folk harp. He asked me what color I wanted and if I wanted decals, and ordered it. This has become the traveling harp. I also have a lap harp that I used to take and play at hospitals and shut-ins and for the dying. I have friends who tell me, "If I am sick, you can visit, but please don't bring your harp. I fear that when you come with your harp that I am dying."

One of our greatest adventures was actually visiting the Lyon and Healy factory in Chicago. It is not easy to get to and is not in an especially desirable part of town, but once you are in, it is a magic land. Harps are made from the bottom floor up. Each stage is done on each floor. Finally at the top you see craftsmen painting on the gold trim of the gorgeous concert harps.

I will share another secret. The harp is not difficult to play. If you can play the piano, you can play the harp. Look under or behind your piano and there is the harp. The harp is just the white keys of the piano and it is actually color-coded. C strings are red and F strings are black. The hardest part is that you have to learn how to make your own repairs and learn how to restring your instrument.

What other lessons have I learned over the years?

First, listen to your children. Sometimes they have a message for you.

My Troubadour harp has thirty-six strings. Again if you play a stringed instrument, you know how you have to keep tuning it. Heat, moisture, anything seems to change the strings, so you are constantly tuning your harp. My husband says I spend half my time, tuning my harp and the other half, playing out of tune. This also is life. If I do not constantly "tune" my relationships with friends, we get out of tune; have trouble relating to each other. When I am with them, we are not "in tune" with each other. All relationships, not just marriages, but relationships with children, friends, co-workers, my God, need constant tuning. I have one friend who calls me every day at approximately the same time in the morning. I see it as a way for us to stay "in tune," and we have become best friends. If only I could be as good at my prayer life.

Along the same lines, I must constantly practice the harp in order to play well. The harp has taught me about tuning, practicing both relationships and music, and how relationships are lost if these two disciplines are forgotten.

I keep my Troubadour at my church where I play each Sunday. My greatest fear is walking in and finding a harp string broken. Putting in a new string is not easy and it takes weeks to get the string stretched enough to stay in tune. Sometimes I try to play without the missing harp string until I have time to fix it. It is amazingly hard to play when just one string is missing even though there is only a small gap between two strings. I know where all the strings are in relationship to the other strings, and when one is missing, I get lost, I can't find my way. Each string is so important, from the shortest to the longest. I cannot play well when just one is missing.

In the last two years I have been taking a course in family systems. I wish I had taken it sooner, just as I wish I had started playing the harp sooner. What I have learned in family systems and in harp playing is that when one relationship in your family is off, I cannot function as well without it, and I must try as much as I can to mend it. We are called to community. This is where we make the best music.

My favorite place to play is outdoors. The place I do this most often is at a chapel on top of Petit Jean Mountain. The wind blows through the strings and makes music. This is my experience in life. When I am outdoors, I realize that there is something greater than my self that is making the music. I think I have forgotten to tell you that you lean the harp against your chest as you play. That means you feel the vibrations of the music in your body and your body is calmed not only by what you hear and touch but also feel. The sound in my ears, the feel of the music of the harp on my fingers and in my body makes me stay in the present, and when I stay in the present connected to something greater than myself, I know "all shall be well, all shall be well, and all shall be well."

Taste and see, and hear, and feel that God is good.
—JJS

Playing the harp at St. Luke's Episcopal Church on Sunday

Praying in Greek

This is a prayer. This is my letter home. Arkansas is a place where I collected clay in a ditch, crushed rocks for paint, and pretended tossed grass clippings were mulch for a garden that grew nothing. Home is a place where thick vines bore the weight of children, and magnolia branches lifted a girl higher and higher until she reached the Aeolian zone, the place of the wind. A leather bottle held water. I carried thick bread in my knapsack. Walking stick in hand, oak and pine forest brought me the scent of earth, creating a memory that continues to surface over time. Home is where quartz showed itself like brilliant teeth half buried in the duff—a sacred treasure for my pocket. And home is where I first heard the stories. The Greek myths my father told me.

Naphlio, Greece: Father's Day 2001. I am a quarter of a century old in this ancient land, rolling with a mythology that shapes its history and growth. There is blood in the land with the scattered sherds. There is healing too, and I find it in the stories.

My thirst for Greek history began as a toddler when my dad read to me from D'aulaire's *Book of Greek Myths.* The leather club chair easily held the two of us with room to spare, but I always curled to his chest, wrapping his arm around me. His hands were a wider version of mine, holding a subtle strength characterized by a surgeon, hands which operated on babies for hours. The readings electrified my imagination and ended with a sense of safety and wonder. Snuggled against my dad, his black beard moving with the words, comfort swept over me, and it was all the world I needed to know.

Twenty years later, polished marble warms our legs as we sit on the steps of the archaeological museum in the peach light of evening. We are waiting for the restaurants to open, hopeful for an authentic Greek meal. The platea slowly fills up with families, rejuvenated from the siesta. A balloon vendor sells mylar animal figures to tourists. We sit and watch the evening light unfold.

In the corner of my eye, I see my dad's peppered beard and large hands opening and closing. His eyes move from his hands to a group of children. They are playing soccer and skirting the platea on push-scooters. Running barefoot on the marble, little brown bodies twist and turn, gallop and race with large, clear eyes. The stucco buildings change hue as the daylight fades—creamy yellow, rusted orange, crumbly red peeking through the bougainvillea.

"I wish I had half their energy," Dad says looking at the children. I feel something turn inside. The thought of savoring grilled octopus becomes a distant interest. I awkwardly offer, "Oh Dad, you are still so young and in good health." He looks ahead in silence watching the children play.

We find a restaurant in an alley with a bougainvillea arbor. Scanning the menu, I see more words than the day before that I am able to read. They rise like Braille, and I confidently tell the waiter, "Horiatiki, ehhhh, octapoda, ehhhh nero parakalo." Dad's order casually rolls off his tongue, even making the facial expression of a native. I have mastered two, full phrases in the two weeks thus far. "Then milo Ellinika," meaning, "I do not speak Greek," and "Efcharisto para poli papakis," meaning "Thank you so very, very much my dear papa."

The waiter asks if we would like any Retsina. "No thank you," Dad says staring at his hands, opening and closing. The knuckles of his fists are white and red.

We eat our meal in silence, absorbing the patrons, the sounds, the cigarette smoke around us. Our attention is suddenly drawn upward as crimson flowers float down to my Greek salad. Bits of straw sprinkle my hair while two cats hiss and chase each other on the arbor. Dad looks at me smiling and effortlessly forms the word I still can't pronounce without tripping over, "Psipsina!" I smile back, attempting the sliding s's with partial success. Dad continues the lesson, "Po, po, po psipsina." "Po, po, po," I echo in my most concerned Greek face.

Walking home, we make our way toward the hotel overlooking the city. Dad grips the iron rail along each set of foot-smoothed staircases reflecting the moonlight. Breathless atop Naphlio, we rest on the Turkish fortification wall enclosing the hotel. Our shadows sit side by side, identical in height. Lights glitter from across the bay of Argos where legend tells of the birth of Perseus. "This time tomorrow, we will be in Santorini, sleeping on the edge of a caldera." "Yeah," I respond, "a sliver of exposed rock from a volcano that swallowed itself in one day. It must be incredible." I take deep breaths searching for the thyme growing in the cracks of the wall. Dad stretches and pats me on the knee as he pushes himself around onto the grass. "Kalinichta Joannamu, don't stay up too late." There is a faint sound of accordions coming from the platea. I close my eyes, and a breeze brings me the scent of jasmine and sweet almond oil.

As Dad goes to sleep, I begin my nightly ritual of staring at his pill bottles in the medicine cabinet. There are three, all of them transparent brown with white caps. The color of the pills are muted dark through the bottle. I begin the label mantra in my head. *Anti-Inflammation Dizziness and/or nausea may occur Do not consume alcohol.*

Five years ago on our trip to Greece, there were no such pills in the medicine cabinet. The bathroom's economic size puts them on display.

I read the labels and stare hard at the pills, but like a language I am learning, only fragments make sense in the midst of utter disorientation.

I can hear Dad's rhythmic breathing from the bathroom, and I pray. I pray for him to sleep as soundly as possible. For there to be no pain in his sleep. Just the pleasure of being in Greece. I pray his hands heal, but deep in the pit of my stomach, I know this is the beginning. I pray for dreams of sharing vine-ripened tomatoes, crisp cucumbers, and thick hunks of feta with my dad. For Kalamata olives and wild thyme.

Taste and see that God is good.
—JESC

Papou's Greek Salad (Horiatiki)
4 large, fresh and ripe tomatoes
3 medium—large cucumbers
Approx. 1 lb. of feta cheese
1 ½ cup of Kalamata olives, pits removed
Fresh or dried oregano to taste
Salt to taste
Olive oil

Slice tomatoes into bite-size wedges. It's not necessary to discard the seeds. Slice cucumbers in half twice, so you have ½ moon-shaped slices. Mix these together in your serving bowl with the olives and enough olive oil to coat the mix. Mix in enough oregano to lightly coat the ingredients. Add salt to taste. Slice the feta cheese in ¼ inch pieces and place them on top of the salad. Sprinkle more oregano on top of the feta. Serve immediately or chill for later use. Avoid putting olive oil on top of the feta as this will cause the cheese to fall apart.

Chapel Imerovigii Santorini Greece   Young Joanna in Greece with her Dad

River Food

Greetings from the place where the Tay and Nashwaak Rivers meet. The confluence of these rivers is the sound I sleep and wake with. I am tenting in a field of timothy, vetch, daisy, and goldenrod between a forest edge and a friend's garden. The trees are alder, birch, spruce, and maple. My visitors are monarchs, hairy spiders, crickets, and lime-green caterpillars. This is a time of rest and meditation, what convention would call a vacation and what I call returning home to a land and people bearing great wisdom and beauty. Taymouth, New Brunswick, is where I farmed organically for two years while finishing my thesis, and it is where I healed from a divorce. I have returned for what locals call being "home from away."

I sleep nestled in a cocoon sleeping bag lent to me by Gordon who lives just up the road. These September nights are in the low 40s, a temperature I last felt in an Arkansas December.

This morning I help Peter in his garden. I carry water from the river, two buckets at a time, to fill large barrels for watering the vegetables. *Madame Butterfly* on CBC's Espace Musique serenades from the car radio while I water parsnips, onions, arugula, and beets. I hold the steel watering can as close to the soil as possible and walk slowly, slowly between the rows, just like I am shown.

Peter gathers a handful of shiny black berries—chockecherries. They are ripe, and clusters hang low over the garden path. I pull the tart fruit off the branches with my mouth and spit the seeds into yarrow and bluebells.

I love watering the garden by hand. I feel connected to centuries of people who cared for the land this way, water from rivers, a river that is the thread in this patchwork quilt of community.

Each morning I follow a ritual: scoop water out of the river into five gallon buckets. Carry them uphill and lift them over my head into blue barrels. Dip the buckets into the barrels and fill the steel watering cans. Follow Peter with the filled buckets to refill the cans. Back and forth I go through waist-high pigweed and lamb's quarter, uneven ground, and an unforgiving sun.

Once we finish four barrels' worth of watering, my only interest is walking into the river, and there I go. I find a pool in front of God and everyone and dive in. The water is an amber, refreshing, swirling, lovingly perfect gift. Trucks and cars pass over the bridge. Someone is hanging laundry out to dry. I swim, float, swish, and dive to my heart's content and feel the stinging places on my skin quiet down.

***

A neighbor friend, Ene, invites me over for supper and homemade wine. I tell her that I gave up alcohol, but I will make an exception for her. Ene's wine is a delicious unlike anything I've tasted before. Perhaps the flavor is enhanced by sitting on the edge of a cliff overlooking the Nashwaak River. Perhaps it is the spring water. The bald eagle nested next to her. Perhaps it is the terraced wildflowers dotting the alpine home she inhabits.

Ene and I swim, tube, and explore the river for hours. It is overcast and chilly, but we are determined. The river is low, so low that the city tubers skip this stretch. When I first arrive in Taymouth, locals are talking about the problem with the tubers on the river. Tubers? There's a problem with potatoes in the river? Carrots?

Two local families have started their own free enterprise business of renting inner-tubes to tourists. A once hidden valley is now visited by a thousand visitors every week. Ene hasn't seen her wildlife friends in months. No sign of beaver, bear, or deer. Bald eagle keeps its perch, and a few mergansers pass through on occasion. That's about it.

Displaced wildlife isn't the only issue. It seems many of the tubers use the river as their personal trash receptacle. Alpine Light beer cans are beginning to pepper the shore. Ene tells me how much she detests seeing the Alpine cans. "Can't they at least have good taste in beer?"

People whose homes border the river have complained about visitors docking off on their land, using their backyard as a toilet, and generally being a nuisance in their screaming and hollering down the rocky stretches. I learn about this last sentiment after I shriek with delight down a 2-foot drop.

The tension over the tubers is palpable. Polarization hasn't settled in yet, but the seeds are there. "This is our neighbor's business. They're trying to make a living, but the river, the river—what about the river?"

There is a valley-wide meeting to discuss constructive steps for addressing concerns. The president of the Nashwaak Watershed Association and other community leaders create an action plan. A committee will be formed along with a Code of Conduct. The RCMP will be invited to help. I want to learn what other communities and local governments have done to manage these challenges. The Blackfoot in Montana is a regular tubing site. Robert Redford couldn't film *A River Runs Through It* on the Blackfoot, where the actual story took place, because the river was so developed and inundated with tourists. My heart breaks at the thought of this secret place turning into a beer can-infested playground.

That's it. I tell a friend we should enlist all of the community artists to create beautiful, hand-painted signs with messages like "Respect Our River" "Know Your River" "Love Our River."

Others in the community have suggested hunkering on the shore and popping the tubes with laser guns, perhaps string some trip wire or maybe a bazooka would help. My Canadian friends are so polite in their morbid suggestions. The ten-year-old in me offers the idea of smacking them with a spud gun. My friend, Andrew, tells me that is a great idea, though he's not sure they'd get the metaphor. Plus, he says it's not really tubing; it's more like blobbing. I should know this from first-hand experience as I float along with Ene.

We circumnavigate the small island she calls Butternut, named for the healthy population of saplings and mature trees. I call it Fiddlehead Island since it is the best place on the river to collect the delicious, gem-like ferns. The western arm of the river is nearly bone dry. We walk on the cobbles, really the river bottom, with our eyes glued to any sign of life. Our only companions are two sandpipers hopping along with us.

Near the fork we stumble upon a goldmine of exposed riverbed. An hour flies by as we comb the polished, gleaming river rocks. Each one is a treasure, a small planet in my hand, a sculpture, a tool, a work of art made by heat and pressure and cold and ice and the sheer force of a still wild river. I tell Ene that I once visited the Smithsonian in D.C. where my only interest was the Museum of Natural History.

"I had a broken leg with a full leg cast. The easiest way of getting around was in a wheel chair, and my dad pushed me everywhere. I insisted on seeing every single rock and mineral in the Museum, and every one I saw. I didn't care about Judy Garland's ruby red slippers. I had to see all of that natural beauty."

"Why didn't you become a geologist, Joanna?"

"I like it all. I wanna learn about it all," I whisper with my face to the rocks.

Ene finds a smooth, oblong rock with lavender and emerald swirls. I find a porous cobble resembling pumice. We cannot resist picking a few to take home, but we have no pockets, bag, or bucket. Instinctively, we drop the stones down our bathing suits. Amidst the colorful rocks are a few bottles and cans. We pick these up too, and again, stuff them down our suits for lack of a better option. Here we are, walking along the river, paddling back up the river in our tubes—two lumpy women brimming with beauty and garbage on a cloudy afternoon.

***

Andrew invites me over for a pool swim. He lives on third-generation land in a house built in 1860. Andrew knows how to use his hands. He's an artisanal woodturner, housebuilder, furniture maker, river golfer, and garden grower with fifteen-foot sunflowers singing to the sky. I arrive prepared for swimming and observe how it's properly done: stand at the top of a grassy knoll, run like mad toward the pool, and leap into the air, hopefully, over the five-foot-tall rim and into the water like a little fish who's found its home. We lounge in the water and relish the coolness while dragonflies skim the surface.

"Are you hungry? Have you had dinner?" Andrew asks.

My standard response to that question without fail is, "I could eat."

I have actually already eaten, but sharing meals with friends in this village is a treasure, and invitations are impossible for me to pass up. "Go ahead and pick through the garden for some veggies." Andrew hands me two small buckets strung together with a wooden board. "It's my berry picking bucket," he says. I pull carrots for a salad.

We walk Gizmo, his short hair border collie, through a path toward the river. Andrew extends his arm in an invitation for me to lead the way. We walk along the old train bed and talk about the river, the ATVers, the dirt bikers, the people who zoom past in their addiction to speed. Andrew is carrying a golf club, a couple of golf balls, an orange ball for Gizmo, and a tee. I'm not sure why exactly.

We wander down to the river at the bend where I've tubed and meditated, skied and explored in the last few years. He places his tee in some stones on a gravel bar, positions the orange ball just so, and whack. Away it goes across the channel, landing on the other side in the Butternut trees. Gizmo charges into the river, the current pushing him as he fights the stream. Then Andrew hits a few golf balls, and one lands in the water. We walk across and find the ball. The whole time we talk about the river and Andrew's frustration with the uproar over the tubers.

"The tubers is just the latest manifestation of what's wrong with the river. People have been dumping garbage and sewage and mistreating the river for years, and suddenly people are upset about it because they can hear all of these people. It's not just the tubers; it's so much more than that. How do we educate all the people who don't show the river respect?" I attempt a thoughtful response. "Well, this may seem a little Pollyannaish, but my inclination is to sit down and have a meal with folks, find out what we have in common, realize that we do indeed share things in common and begin to build trust and communication from there."

Andrew's expression is something along the lines of *you really are crazy, aren't you?* Instead, he says, "I don't have two to four years to build those relationships. Something needs to be done now. We need a code of conduct, and we need enforcers."

Yes, there are short-term solutions and long-term perspectives. I think it's possible to have both. That is the hope.

There is a flowering shrub in full bloom along one of the gravel bars, and I ask Andrew if he knows this plant. "I've noticed it growing along the river, and it is so beautiful that I wonder if it's native. Any time I see something so striking, I worry it's nonnative and an escapee from an avid gardener."

The orange and yellow blossoms are exquisite.

"You don't know this plant, Joanna? I can't believe you don't know this. It's called Touch-Me-Not. Come here and I'll show you why."

"Okay."

"Here, you see this dangling little pod? Well, just gently let it rest in your palm."

"Oh, okay." Within seconds, the pod explodes in my face, and I shriek. "Wow—How amazing! Do it again, show me again!"

We return to Andrew's house to his pool for another dip just after sunset. I welcome the chlorinated water knowing that this is the closest my camping-river-Atlantic Ocean-swimming body is getting to a proper bath. There is a chill settling in, and as soon as we get out of the water, the evening air is a shock. Andrew shrieks, "Ah—it's so cold—" He runs into his house, up the staircase and into the shower. I change into warmer clothes behind the garage.

While Andrew showers, I wash carrots. The Dave Matthews Band fills the entire house.

He comes down and says, "Joanna, do yourself a favor and go upstairs and take a bath in my claw-foot tub. I have bath salts. Knock yourself out." He says this as if I am doing him a favor. My legs are rockets on the staircase. Music and warm water surround me, and I feel a long-ago comfort, something I have trouble naming but know it has something akin to feeling held.

I am bathed and refreshed. Andrew prepares a meal of grilled vegetables and steaks. A new friend, Justin, stops by for a visit, and the three of us devour our food slowly on Andrew's screened porch. "What is it about swimming that makes you feel like you could eat a horse?" I ask.

We talk for hours about the village, the history of the valley, families who've worked this land and earned it for generations. They are still here. We talk about travel adventures and mishaps, the world-altering effects of typhoid fever, and dreams: the power they hold and how we are surrounded by synchronicity all the time. We just need to open our eyes and spirits. I tell Andrew that there is something magical about this valley, this village. There is something particularly special. "The people here share this certain kind of deep spirituality without really being religious."

Andrew raises his arm and points west. "It's the river, Joanna. The river is the thread."

And then it hits me. The river and the land are woven into the people here, whether or not they realize this. Whether or not they have a livelihood dependent upon the land or a culture of tradition connected to the land. The land and water is an extension, an expression, a vehicle, a medium for the people who make their home here. The Maliseet say that when the Anglos dammed their river, they dammed their language. Taymouth isn't immune from the unfortunate choices made on the land, but each morning the river is still there to greet, to hold, and to teach us what we have in common.

Taste and see that God is good.
—JESC

Nashwaak River

Menu for a 100-Mile Race

In October of 2013 our oldest son, Rob, ran in the Arkansas Traveler 100 Mile Race. The route is on trails up and down hills around Lake Sylvia in the Ouachita National Forest. Rob is in his early forties and has been training for a year for the rugged race. We followed the race on a web site that told us every few hours where he was. One hundred and one runners started the race and eighty finished. Racers came from all over the country with two runners from Japan. The youngest runner was twenty-two and the oldest was seventy. Seventy. I cannot imagine that. This is my age.

I asked Rob about the food before and during the race. He replied, "I ate lots of protein before the race: thick, rich burgers, sweet potato fries, white truffle and pecorino burgers from a local upscale burger restaurant called Big Orange. During the race every four to five miles there were aid stations with wonderful food. The weather was cold and rainy for at least half of the race so I ate lots of soup, chicken noodle and potato soup. There were incredible grilled cheese sandwiches, salted potatoes, hot cocoa, coffee, and quesadillas. When I got tired of soup I ate peanut butter and crackers. At the last aid station called Pumpkin Patch at mile ninety-five I had pumpkin pie."

I wondered how in the world could someone do this. Rob said, "A friend told me that when you think about it, one hundred miles isn't very far. You don't have to run fast, just run all day. Of course it took me more than a day. Another thing I heard that helped me along the way was, 'it never gets worse.'"

Rob attributes finishing the race to a community of friends who encouraged and walked and ran with him. "I had a friend who crewed for me at some of the first aid stations, mile sixteen and mile thirty-one, as well as some of the later stations. She was there to help me with anything I needed: a change of wet socks and clothes, putting a bandage on a possible blister, getting any aid food I needed, making sure I brought any extra food with me. She was truly incredible and had one of the most thankless jobs because she was waiting for most of the day, just for me. I would only see her for about five to ten minutes at a time and she would move on. Of course she was there at the finish for me as well. I also had three pacers, people who came and ran or walked with me from mile forty-eight to sixty-eight, from sixty-eight to eighty-three, and then from eighty-three to the finish. By the time I picked up my first pacer at mile forty-eight, I knew I could finish the race. I just had to keep moving. Don't sit down, and stay away from a chair or a warm fire. I knew whether it was running, power walking hiking, or gingerly walking or shuffling, I was going to finish. It was a pretty amazing sight to see those marker every five miles, just to see those miles tick off: sixty, sixty-five, seventy, seventy-five. My pacers helped me just get through. Towards the end by mile seventy-five or so, I wasn't doing a lot of running. It just helped to have someone talk to me and be with me. I still don't know how those solo runners do it, especially at night. Because of my pacers, I never went to the *dark place* where my mind starts to *talk* to me and tell me how I could easily drop out. My pacers were with me during what some may say is the hardest part of a hundred miler—the night time."

As Rob's dad and I followed the race, we were amazed at the number of people who dropped out when they were at mile eighty-five, so close to the finish. Rob answered, "Again that was perhaps the most rugged part of the race. I could have never made it without my friends."

Another more experienced runner, Scott Brockmeier, wrote on his blog about meeting Rob in the race.

It was about mid-morning when the rain started. It was a nice gentle drizzle at first but we could hear the thunder off in the distance and it wasn't long before the skies opened up. The rain came dumping down and the temps dropped dramatically. I had been debating on whether I should carry my rain jacket because it really wasn't that cold at the start but I was glad I had it in this tempest. While running along a guy caught up with me that did not have a jacket and we started to chat. His name was Rob Seibert, and he was cold. He was a first time one hundred miler and I could tell talking to him that he was worried about his race. He asked me how many times I had done the race and how he wouldn't see his crew for a while and how cold he was getting. I told him that he was young and strong and fit and that he would get through this speedbump and feel just fine later. I told him they would likely have some extra trash bags to make a poncho at the next aid station and that as long as he kept moving he'd be fine.

As we talked, I mentioned Hardrock and Rob asked me if I knew a guy named Billy Simpson. Well, well. It turns out that my old friend Billy had been informally coaching Rob and I knew now that I had to make sure that Rob finished this thing. We continued to run together for a while and I tried to give him as much help and motivation and confidence as I could. I gave him the "quitting is not an option" speech and felt pretty sure that he would tough it out. He had crew and pacers later in the race and it sounded like they had experience and would not easily let him quit.

At the next aid station they were in full on garbage bag poncho production. It seemed like half the people leaving that aid station were wearing black plastic bags. Just another example of how well prepared these folks were.

Many of the aid stations had been manned by the same groups for many years, and it really showed. The food selection was excellent, they were good about helping you get in and out quickly, and many were runners themselves which always makes a difference. I don't remember when Rob and I split paths but it was after the fifty mile mark. After I finished we hung out at the finish enjoying the nice pancake/bacon/egg breakfast and watching folks come in. I asked about Rob and found that he was in fact going to finish and introduced myself to his crew person and his wife who had only arrived that morning. It was an emotional finish for him and fun to watch him succeed at his first one hundred mile attempt. It was hard and he was sore and whupped but he did it. Good job Rob!

Rob started at 6 am Saturday and finished twenty-eight hours and twenty-five minutes later at 10:25a.m. Sunday morning. At the finish line, Mary Anne, Rob's wife wrote, "There is no way I can even try to describe the emotion, so I'll leave it at that."

Rob later wrote, "It is still hard to believe that I did it. Someone else told me that as the years go on, you will be amazed that you ever did such a thing. I guess it takes a while to settle in."

I asked him what were some of his thoughts during the race. Rob waited a moment and said, "What did I think about during the one hundred miler? As someone else has said, I thought about everything and nothing."

It took Rob some time to recover from the race. When he did, his family threw an adult and children's party at his home for all those who helped him, serving Arkansas-style chili, barbeque, and carrot cake for dessert as they all celebrated this victory together. Whenever you ask Rob about his race, he usually doesn't talk about what it was like for him, but instead about how it takes a village for one Arkansas Traveler to run and walk one hundred miles.

Taste and see that God is good.
—JJS

Rob and his son Turner at the Firecracker Race

Lunch on Your Personal Day,
The Next Right Thing

I am home on Friday, my Personal Day, having my favorite garden salad from Boulevard Bakery. Friday is the day I try to sleep in late, walk in the pool, and renew my soul. The call comes from Joe. Terry's procedure is not going well. He doesn't directly ask me to come, but says, "I remember someone else who had this procedure and it did not go well." This is a sign. I know I need to go. I slowly finish my lunch trying to work on a plan of how and where to go in the hospital. It is harder for me to make hospital visits since having trouble with my legs from a back surgery, but I know I need to go. Robert takes me over to St. Vincent's on his way to Children's Hospital for a meeting. Joe does not know which floor he is on or where he is in the hospital. He thinks it is near cardiac cath. I know where that is. It is on the second floor just off the elevators. I get off the elevators on the second floor. No Joe. I call him and he still sees a sign for cardiac cath, but he must be seeing a different sign. I go into the cardiac cath area and see two men coming out of the restricted cath doors. I ask, "Do you know where special procedures cath area is?"

One of the men is a physician, I think a cardiologist. He never makes eye contact, shakes his head, and says he does not know. The other appears to be a nuclear medicine technologist for he is carrying material in a lead holder.

"I know. Follow me," says the technologist.

He walks with a limp as we go all the way to the other side of the hospital, down one floor, and into the bowels of radiology.

"You are having as much trouble walking as I do," I say as I slowly follow him, each step with my quad cane that has become a permanent part of my body.

"I have had one knee replacement, and need to have the other," he replies not missing a beat and still carrying the lead-lined container.

Finally we are there. I see Joe. I thank my guide and bless him, even though deacons aren't supposed to bless.

Terry's procedure is being done by one of my former residents. I remember him as much younger. Now I wish I had spent more time with him. He seems very competent and the procedure goes well. Later we go with Terry after his procedure to the outpatient surgery recovery area. Debbi Fricks, a choir member and director of the bell choirs at St. Luke's is one of the nurses working there. I had no idea this is where she worked. She greets me with, "We are looking forward to seeing you Monday." I am having outpatient surgery Monday. She tells me what to expect. This quiets some of my anxiety about the surgery. Terry is doing well and is starting to look like his old self.

As I ponder the day I see how God feeds my soul every day, but maybe especially on a personal day. For some reason a voice tells me what "the next right thing" to do is. I change my agenda and follow that voice. When I become lost, suddenly there appears another person who also hears a voice about doing the "next right thing," which is not so easy for him to do. I am embarrassed, for I have already forgotten his name. I am led to be present with two old friends. I don't know if my being there was helpful to them, but it was helpful to me to see things going well, and by some miracle I meet someone else I know who is present in that place to comfort and care for me.

Taste and see that God is good.
—JJS

There Is Room for Everyone at the Table

The Spiritual Meaning of Delicious

As the wood smoke begins to fill the room, the damp chill from the mountain air is slowly overtaken by the warmth of a small fire crackling in the center of the floor. The room is small, made of dark wood, and full of Tujia people gathered to hear the American's questions. We huddle around the fire-pit with smoke circling upward to blackened hunks of pork hanging from iron hooks. Cups of green tea circulate, and cigarettes are offered just as freely. A kitten finds something worth licking on the sole of my shoe. With a tear of gray light peering from the only window in the room, we squint our eyes as the smoke finds our faces, we smile, sip tea, puff on our cigarettes, and through all of this, begin a form of communion.

My friend, Li Weichang, is my translator and colleague. We met seven years ago at an international family forest conference. Now we are in a remote mountain village in southern Hubei, China, where I am the first white female most villagers have seen. On top of that, I'm five-foot-eleven. On the walk to this home, women come up to me, touch my arm, and with smiling bright eyes, squeeze my left hand with their left hand. This is the hand that leads straight to the heart.

I have come to this village in Hubei because it is a place that has somehow managed to keep much of its culture intact. People still know how to grow their own food, cook amazing dishes, and hold people who know the land in high regard.

"I am from Arkansas, USA. Where I come from, I did not learn how to grow food. I did not learn how to cook. Most people do not know how to grow food and cook where I am from," I say with a sudden embarrassment in my attempt for simple, clear communication. There is no time for whitewashing American culture or going into complicated sociological and political explanations. It doesn't occur to me to explain that Arkansas is actually an agricultural state, because this would force further translation complications. For instance, what is agriculture, then, when the focus is on industrially grown commodities with little consideration for the soil and ecological economics of the place? Plain and simple—most of us are products of a severed connection with food, farming, and land, hence knowing who we are.

Many of the people giggle when this is translated. The expressions give off an incredulousness that seems to say, *How can that be true? That doesn't make any sense?* And all there is to do is laugh a little.

I ask the village leader if they have a problem with young people leaving the community for bigger cities.

"Yes," he says.

"Are you worried about this?" I ask.

"Yes, but we know they will come back."

"Are you confident your village will be able to grow its own food in the future?"

"Oh, yes."

"What about the young people? If they have left the farming life, how will they know how to grow food when they return?"

"They will remember. We will help them remember."

"You are rich," I say. "You know so much of what we have lost. You have so much knowledge of how to look after your bodies and land. You are so rich. You have a wealth most of us have never known."

Li Weichang tells me that he's worried this sentiment of young people returning is wishful thinking within the village. They have lived with abundance for so long in their fertile soil, healthy forests full of medicine, clean water and air, and a breathtaking landscape. Global problems and temptations are beginning to skirt the edges of this village. I realize there may be more in common with this pocket of 300 people and the whole of North America.

In only two generations, most North Americans have lost the knowledge of how to grow food sustainably. The consequences of such a short break are presenting Herculean challenges to regain some sensibility in how we relate to the land, each other, and our selves. We are now faced with a universal question: Where will the next generation of farmers come from?

***

Hands down, the most delicious meal in China is in the tiny kitchen of this Tujia home. We migrate from the smokehouse living room to a round table where eight of us squeeze together on squat wooden chairs. A thick fabric circles the table. We gather the material onto our laps so that we may feel the warmth of coals burning in a small saucer at our feet. The family cooking for us fills the table with steaming dishes of roasted green chilies, tofu from their gristmill, homemade potato chips sprinkled with sugar cane, mouth-watering smoked pork, chicken with heaps of garlic and ginger in a bubbling broth, an unidentified tingling medicine dish, and rounds of more tea from the hillsides holding their homes. Through the steam, we toast each other—to making new friends, to good health and good soil. I have learned the word for "delicious" and each time I say this, more food appears from the biofuel stove. This is a thanksgiving like no other in a room barely held by wooden walls, in a room full of people who know who they are and the land they are part of.

Dizzy from the fellowship, food, and mountain tea, I am overcome with only what I can call Agape. Love for all with no expectation or strings attached. Love in the present moment. Acceptance for myself and love for what each person brings to this little table swelling with good food. I want this moment to last forever—to ride this feeling like an ocean wave all the way back to Arkansas and stitch our land and communities back together. The toast I want to offer goes unspoken, but it is there inside along with the love for this moment. "Do not make our mistakes," I want to say. "Do not try to be like us. Hold on to what you have. Your wealth is immeasurable."

I do not say this.

Instead, I lift my cup. "Delicious."

Taste and see that God is good.
—JESC

China diet

How I Got Over Being a Radical Foodie Southern Health Nut

One of my vexing habits is collecting ideas on what I believe is right and true. Friends are patient with these declarations, and in their gentle ways, try to teach me the difference between wisdom and dogma. I'm still learning how to discern between life-giving and more narrow ways of thinking. I've gathered bits of knowledge that form my list of truths. Here is an example:

- Healthy soil equals healthy communities.
- Soil is the common denominator. If you don't have healthy soil, it's not long until you reach the limits of technocratic approaches to agriculture.
- If local movements are going to survive, people need to know how to cook, reacquaint themselves with their kitchens, and share meals with friends and family.
- Food is medicine.

This last bit, "Food is medicine," is something I tangibly experienced on my first trip to China. Countless meals involved foods my Chinese friends did not know the English word for. The only translation they could offer was *medicine*. Sometimes I could tell the food was some kind of fungi or the obvious shape of garlic and ginger. These edibles are a staple in most Chinese dishes. I haven't formally researched the Chinese concept of health and medicine; I only know my experience of eating with people in multiple provinces where each meal is a medicinal feast. Whether being treated to an elaborate banquet in a fancy hotel or huddling around a rickety table high up in the mountains, I experienced each meal with sensory delight and chock-full of ingredients they called medicine. It was delicious, flavorful food.

The rare occasions where I stayed in a western hotel in China and was served western food felt like culinary torture. I didn't want the yucky white flour soupy pancakes. I wanted my bubbling dish of spicy peppers, heaps of garlic, and roasted chicken. Give me lotus roots and wasp larvae any day over mushy pasta.

My month of eating medicine each day changed my food paradigm and my body. My clothes loosened, which was a mystery because I had filled my belly every day of my trip. I learned that each time I said the Mandarin word for "delicious" more food miraculously appeared. I ate and ate and drank pints of earthy green tea. I realized that I hadn't been eating my Southern staples of refined sugar, coffee, white flour, and processed foods. I wondered what it would be like to continue eating as if I were in China. This birthed what became known in my family as the China Diet. I don't like the word, diet, because it connotes making a significant change only for a short period of time. It feels like a false promise glorified by a short-term Band-Aid. Instead, my direct experience was changing the way I looked at food and food choices over time. I cut out alcohol, caffeine, all processed foods, white flour, most dairy, and refined sugar. I lost more weight and felt I had finally discovered a sustainable way of eating and being healthy. Plus, I enjoyed sharing this story with anyone who would listen. Come hear the gospel according to Joanna.

On one occasion I was at a local food banquet in Chattanooga, Tennessee. I had driven a dozen of the AmeriCorps members serving at the nonprofit I was working for on Petit Jean Mountain just outside Little Rock. We were attending a well-known Southern sustainable agriculture conference and soaking up all of the workshops, stories, and emerging social networks. It's an exciting time to be a sustainable farmer in the South. At the banquet, a striking young woman from Brazil joined our table. Our conversation eventually led to food, and I shared with her my experience in China and the radical shift I made in how I think of food and how I eat. She listened intently, then pausing for a few seconds, she responded, "You know, I don't think I could do what you're doing. I would feel sadness in my heart. I would miss the foods from my family traditions and my culture. It would hurt too much to give up these experiences."

Her words hit me like a shock wave. Wow. Family traditions. Cultural foods. Feeling a heart connection to these foods and a longing. Wow. What are the cultural foods from my family? My mom stopped cooking in 1982, says it was the best decision she ever made. So, I grew up knowing diddly-squat about how to combine ingredients, much less feel a connection between the meal, the place, and the people. Does Western Sizzlin' count? Red Lobster? Holidays became our landmarks for creating special meals together at home. I treasure these memories of rockfish, pecan pie, and my brother's lentil soup. My Brazilian dinner companion described a different world, shedding light on a curious culinary landscape. It wasn't just about food and sustenance. *Every* meal was a celebration of her family and traditions, sharing in something special together each day, not just on special occasions. I carried her words with me for a few more years, continuing on with my China outlook and not entirely sure of how to integrate her wisdom into my own place in the southern United States. I wasn't prepared to start eating fried chicken and hushpuppies, both iconic Southern foods. And what good role models do us food-weary

Southerners have for ways of cooking? Paula Dean? I dare not tread down that road.

All of my well-crafted righteous ways of living came crashing to a halt the day my husband showed up in my life. Dennis comes from a small town in eastern Arkansas, in the Mississippi delta. His grandparents were sharecroppers. Alongside the cotton and soybeans grew a vegetable garden that Dennis' grandfather cast prayers over each season. Dennis was raised on collard greens, pinto beans, black-eyed peas, and cornbread alongside sun-ripened peaches, sweet corn, and okra. He knew the world of heirloom tomatoes before tomato-tasting festivals were hip, and he makes the best cornbread I have ever tasted. One of the results of marrying him is that I've turned into a cornbread snob. I admit it, even turning my nose up at restaurants claiming to serve Southern food. You don't add sugar and white flour to cornmeal. You just don't. I now know what good cornbread tastes like.

To say that Dennis loves food and loves to cook is an understatement. Before we've finished lunch, he's asking me what I want for dinner. With a fridge full of prepared food, he begins cooking more meals because, as he says, "I just need to cook something." On a bad day, he says, "I need to cook something." On a good day, he says, "Honey, I need to cook something." Picture Mark Twain with darker hair at the stovetop.

My introverted self watches in amazement. There must be a cooking gene, and he's got it etched firmly in his genetic code. When we moved in together, I wondered how my China Diet would fit with Dennis' ways. Should I insist on only local, organic, shade grown, non-processed, no sugar, no caffeine, fair trade, bird friendly, and so on?

As if God whispered directly in my ear, I heard the words, "Good Lord, girl, if you want your marriage to be good and have fun, you've gotta lighten up."

"You gotta taste this," Dennis says as he hands me a wooden spoon steaming with homemade gumbo. It is perfection. "The secret to good gumbo is a good roux," he says, "It's got to look like a dirty copper penny." As Dennis shells the Gulf Coast shrimp for the pot, he grins and exclaims, "I'm so good at this, I can't stop." Lucky for me.

Once I tasted Dennis' cornbread, I felt a pull in my body. My heart traveled from China to a territory traced by delighting in cultural traditions my own family lost track of before I was born. Traditions close to the land I call home. Traditions rooted in generations farming dark loamy soil. Of ceramic bowls holding succulent strawberries and sweet, raw onion on my tongue. Of pickled peppers on beans and tomato gravy on biscuits. The Chinese call it *medicine*. Dennis' family calls it *good food*. While I still care about where my food comes from, I'm also learning the value of not fussing so much about how healthy I'm being, of savoring the incredible foods my Southern River Delta husband prepares. I can't imagine my world without his cooking. There would be sadness in my heart. It would hurt too much.

Taste and see that God is good.
—JESC

Dennis' Re-Sanctified Cornbread Recipe
2 cups stoneground cornmeal
1 tsp baking powder
1 tsp baking soda
1 tsp salt
3 large eggs
2 cups of buttermilk
3 Tbsp Sriracha Sauce
1 can of Rotel
1 Tbsp minced garlic
1 cup Vidalia Onions
8 oz Smoked Bacon Bits and Ends
2 Tbsp bacon grease

Pre-heat cast-iron skillet and oven at 450 degrees
Mix cornmeal, baking powder, baking soda and salt
Blend buttermilk with Sriracha Sauce
Saute onions and garlic
Cook and then crumble bacon
Mix everything together including bacon grease
Oil pan with bacon grease
Pour complete mixture into pre-heated skillet
Bake for approximately 25 minutes

Eat three slices and you will be re-sanctified, eat six and you'll never backslide again.

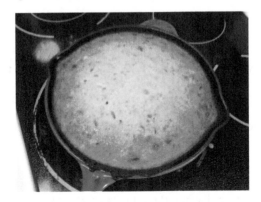

Prayers of Thanksgiving

Day 1

Eat breakfast at the High Spot café. Order a latte and the Berkley bowl.
Walk to Epiphany church and see the houses along the way.
They are planted on steep ridges creeping with ivy.
Feel the sun. Feel the shade. Feel the cool.
Touch the lavender and rosemary breaking up the sidewalk.
Come home to watch your favorite show—this time, it's *Mad Men*.
Curl up with the blanket you knitted years ago.
Nap.
Work out at the gym.
Go to dinner at the hole-in-the-wall Thai place.
You like the jazz they play on the stereo.
Talk about church politics.
Continue to be amazed by the stories of how fragile even clergy are.
Go to the Lake. Look out across the water. To Mercer and Bellevue.
The floating bridge. Watch the sailboats coasting by at sunset.
The old man fishing on the pier.
Share more stories. Find the nearest coffee shop for another latte.
Pick up milk and juice at the market next door.
Share the load as we each carry a jug and return home to the rectory.

Day 2

Find Discovery Park. Wander through the grandmother trees—the green, new life forming on decay.
Walk into the water at low tide. Take pictures of anemones and barnacles.
Feel gratitude for the simplicity of Saltine crackers.

Day 3

Picnic on the bed—red wine, three kinds of cheese, bread, olive oil, olives, salami, dark chocolate—and more of your favorite show.
Step outside before going to bed—breathe and take in
The Big Dipper—it's really there.

The downtown skyline.
Breathe in the cool air once more—
A new landscape, a new language, customs, ecology, LOVE.
Breathe.

—JESC

Revolving Tables Restaurant

We stop for lunch on the way to the beach at one of our favorite restaurants, The Revolving Tables, an "all you can eat" family style restaurant in the Old Mendenhall Hotel in a small town outside of Jackson, Mississippi. The food is placed on a large Lazy Susan in the middle of each table which accommodates approximately twelve people. Every day they serve down-home freshly cooked vegetables, rolls and corn bread, and catfish and ham the way your grandmother cooked them for Sunday dinner. You quickly learn the art of catching food as it whizzes by on the large lazy Susan at your table. Similar to a Japanese steakhouse, you may sit with strangers if you didn't bring eleven other people with you.

Mississippi has as many interesting people as Arkansas. This time we sit across the revolving table from the minister, his wife, and a deacon and his wife from a local Baptist church. The minister's wife was very proud of her husband. When she introduced herself to the gentleman next to her, she made it very clear which Baptist church and how large a church her husband led. I immediately thought, *Not another one of those. One more woman living her life through her husband.*

Through the course of the meal, with true Southern style, the preacher's wife related by eye contact with each one of us at the table. I waited my turn. I knew what to expect. I was anticipating that special smile I had grown up with, that look that I also knew how to emulate. But when it came my turn, as she replaced the creamed corn and butter beans I was waiting for, her smile was not that Pollyanna pious Southern syrup I expected. When she looked my way, to borrow from Wesley, "I felt my heart strangely warmed." Her gaze was compassionate, not sentimental. It was an *I've been there, too* look. Her expression reminded me of the people in the last scene from the movie *Places in the Heart* when the peace is passed during communion in church where all of the characters, living and dead, are now reunited in a common bond of love.

I do not know how you smile "the peace of God" to someone, but the preacher's wife expressed it to me. I felt her eyes, her mouth, her cheeks saying to me, *Namastè: I see God inside you, and I rejoice in it.* I suddenly remembered receiving that look often in my past from another preacher's wife, my grandmother.

We smiled at each other several times. I never introduced myself or heard her name. I don't know what this encounter meant to the preacher's wife, but I felt loved and accepted by this woman I will never know.

Here we were, two very different women in our goals, our lifestyle, and our relationship with God; and yet we were able to see, receive, and transmit God in each other. I felt a glimmer of hope that if two dissimilar Southern women could accept each other, for a brief moment in time there was an expectation that we all might make a connection with God within each of us and maybe even expand it into several minutes or even longer. I especially felt hope that my judgmental prejudices might be healed and transformed by the God who made and loves us all.

Taste and see that God is good.
—JJS

Revolving Tables Restaurant in Mendenhall, Mississippi

Two Parties at Children's Hospital

I so well remember the day my husband retired from his medical practice and his patients returned to say thank you and good-bye at a grand party at Children's Hospital. His primary work had been operating on children with cleft palates and lips, restoring these children to a life of beauty and hope. It was so moving to see the gratitude of these children and their parents for his work. I treasure the picture of him with these patients at his retirement eating cake and ice cream.

I knew this was an experience that I would only know secondhand, through him, for my medical specialty is pediatric radiology. Most of the patients I help never know or see me or the work I have done to help restore them to health. It is the downside of being in a medical specialty where you deal more directly with other physicians than with patients.

However, I had a monumental experience recently when as I attended the twenty-fifth birthday party of the neonatal unit at Arkansas Children's Hospital. I had been at Children's when the neonatal intensive care unit was born. Patients and their parents who had been cared for in this intensive care unit returned to celebrate this great anniversary. I was in a room filled with cake and cookies and children, most of whose X-rays I had read, on whom I had performed many procedures. Some I knew I had helped care for and diagnose their condition. The children and their parents would not know me, and I would never know them. Most of my prayers for them had been in secret, as I learned to know their inner being only in the black and white of their X-rays. But there was an overwhelming feeling of being in a room full of people whom I had known intimately and had in some small way walked beside on a journey in the first days of their lives. Perhaps sometimes I helped them, restored them to life or had given them a new life. We would never know each other.

I knew life had some meaning as I saw these children, many now adults. I cried with joy. I thought of so many other hidden employees of this hospital who have made a difference in lives by simply doing the job they were given: housekeepers, pharmacists, operating room nurses, and helicopter pilots that these families would never know. I knew God had used all of us for a purpose, often when we had forgotten about it or were unaware. It did not matter that we did not recognize each other.

We had a beautiful secret bond of helping each other on this journey and I felt so grateful that we had secretly known each other.

Taste and see that God is good.
—JJS

Mothering Tea: My New Life As a Priest's Wife

A Sunday doesn't pass without remembering the advice Beth Maze offered about becoming a priest's wife.

1. There is no job description.
2. Watch out for both the negative and positive projections because they're both dangerous.
3. Be yourself ten times over.

Beth is a bishop's wife, so I take her words seriously. The list is good wisdom, and it's carried me through the few awkward moments so far at St. Clement Episcopal Church, the first church where my membership includes the role of "clergy spouse." I couldn't have anticipated how much her advice prepared me for the annual Mothering Tea, a tradition the Episcopal Church Women (ECW) have kept going for decades.

The ECW has a knack for decorating the Parish Hall. They are a hodgepodge collection of gifted women who turn the basement that periodically floods into a whimsical, charming room with potted herbs, pastel streamers, and tables adorned with old and new tea china, some matching, some not. There is an African table with lions on plates and a gourd thumb piano. One table has a child's accordion and ocarina, a wind instrument. This year's Mothering Tea is titled "Joyful Noise" to celebrate the diverse musical offerings within the church. There is the Mt. Baker Neighborhood Children's Choir, the Byrd Ensemble, violin lessons, and of course, the St. Clement Choir. Music comprises a hefty chunk of the church's budget, so as one vestry member says, "We're paying all of this money for all of this music; I guess we gotta do *something* for it."

Becoming a clergy spouse is only the beginning of what is new for me. St. Clement is a racially diverse Anglo-Catholic parish, which I'm told would be the envy of many Episcopal clergy who dream about diversity beyond their one or two families of color. *Lift Every Voice*, a popular black gospel hymnal, has as much significance as the *1982 Hymnal*. Diversity mixed with the Anglo-Catholic practices of singing nearly every spoken word is refreshingly different from the mostly white Episcopal parishes I attended growing up in Little Rock, Arkansas. These churches of my youth were full of people whom I looked up to as positive, iconic figures for Episcopal identity, but the lack of singing, I realize now, was as sterile as the unleavened communion wafers that would often stick to the roof of my mouth. Tack on Seattle, and we are suddenly the odd balls for being Christian in the most secular city in the United States. Perhaps this is why the women in the church are fascinating to me. Their Pacific Northwest ethos of each person's right to be who she is makes the extraordinary become ordinary each Sunday morning. It's okay to be strange, funky, eccentric, artistic, conservative, wildly liberal, gay, straight, transgendered, or any identity you're capable of creating as long as it's done without harm to others. This is more than a galaxy away from the days of wearing floral print dresses purchased at Laura Ashley.

Three months into being a clergy spouse, the women of St. Clement still go out of their way to make me feel welcome. I appreciate their warmth and colorful personalities. They are just as interesting and diverse as the creative assortment of china displayed for the tea.

When I arrive, I am greeted by tables covered in platters of homemade cookies, fudge, and tarts. Little sandwiches with the crusts cut off. The teapots are shaped like pianos, overweight farmers, and flowerpots. There is a wedding teapot with a music box in the bottom.

Nikki introduces herself to me. She has two granddaughters in tow, one nine, the other eleven. Nikki wears layers of sparkly shirts and a funky scarf that doesn't come close to matching; her fingernails are painted pink with little white flowers. I immediately decide to sit next to her. I remember pretending teatime with my young nieces and how sweet and playful they were sipping from the miniature pewter cups and nibbling their digestive biscuits. I think to myself, *This is great. I get to play tea with a grandmother and her darling girls.*

Diane joins us at the table, followed by Paul. The extent of my friendship with both people began with unforeseen hospitality on their part. As a result of overhearing a passing comment about my size eleven feet, Diane leans over a pew during this morning's service to hand me a shoe catalogue specializing in plus-size footwear for women. "Gosh, thanks so much," I whisper. "Yeah," she says, "Otherwise, you'd have to go to Brazil where there are larger shoes for women because of all the transvestites." I appreciate the gesture. Paul knows that I like to knit, hike, and eat collard greens and has made a college effort to educate me on where to buy yarn, walk, and shop for the best groceries in town. Again, I'm grateful.

I usually appreciate any opportunity to talk with young people. The eldest, Arianna, has braces, and her bangs are died green. She is turning twelve this week. Her sister, Katy, waxes happily about Justin Bieber, and in particular, his hair—the way it swishes to one side. Nikki discusses her Swedish roots and the pancake breakfast each Sunday at the Swedish Cultural Center. Nikki's accent is melodic, and I ask her if she grew up in Sweden. "Oh no. It was my great grandparents. But Seattle has a lot of Scandinavian blood. Anymore, it's all Scando-Asian." From there the discussion leaves any semblance of what I was taught to discuss in Parish Halls, even an Episcopal one.

Out of the blue, Nikki exclaims, "I caught some of my Saudi students going into Hooters the other day."

"That's where women go to work in their underwear, right?" I jokingly ask.

"Oh no," Paul says, "It's just really tight shirts and shorts. They're not that scantily clad, and there's no dancing on tables."

"Were these students underage?"

Matter-of-factly, Nicki says, "No, they were all over twenty-one. They said they were there for a cultural experience."

"Well, for a cultural experience," I say, "they could just open the *Seattle Weekly.*"

All the adults around the table make a huffing sound indicating their disapproval of the paper.

"That's just junk," Nikki says. "All those lurid ads."

Diane shares her perspective, "The writing is pretty boring. I think people must look at it for the pictures."

"Well, never mind the pictures and ads," I say. "In Arkansas, we don't have articles devoted to medical marijuana farmers' markets and reviews on the quality of cannabis varieties." There are nods of agreement.

In an effort to steer the conversation to a more tea-wholesomeness, I ask Arianna what she has planned for her birthday.

Laconically, she shares, "Oh, I'm gonna have a party and watch movies."

"Oh, how fun," I exclaim. "What movies are you going to watch?"

Under her breath, Nikki says, "Probably *Deep Throat.*"

It takes me about thirty seconds to register this comment. Did I really just hear that? I look at Paul, and his expression mirrors the bewildered look on my face. I look back to Nikki, and without skipping a beat, she follows her train of thought with, "Well, you just never know what kids are into these days."

Uh, yeah. They're into Justin Bieber.

"Okay, okay. I am not going to give up here," I think to myself.

"So, wasn't the *King's Speech* great?" I ask.

"Oh, yes," both girls exclaim. "Who wouldn't like anything with Colin Firth?" Diane reveals. She continues. "But, *Black Swan* was just too weird for my taste. I mean, that scene where she's having sex with the other girl. It was getting so strange, I was sure a dog was going to enter the scene and they would start practicing bestiality."

"Um, well, I," pausing, I come up with, "Do you think these cookies are organic?"

In a last ditch effort, I ask Arianna if she's reading any good books. She loved Colin Firth in *Pride and Prejudice*, and I wonder if she's enjoyed Jane Austen.

"I like C*rank*," she says.

"*Crank*? What's that about?"

"Drugs."'

"Making drugs?" I ask.

"No. How drugs mess up your life."

"Oh, yeah…yep, they sure do."

Arianna and Katy look increasingly bored by the conversation. Nikki tells her grandchildren to ask me what just recently happened to my husband. "Go on, ask her. Ask Joanna what just happened to Father Dennis. He almost died, you know."

"Well, he got this spider bite," I begin to share, "A brown recluse. It has the kind of venom that eats away at your flesh and…" Arianna stops me, sits upright with her hand raised and exclaims, "No, not at tea. Not that kind of talk."

Oh, I see. All the other stuff was okay. Hooters, pornography, bestiality, and drugs are acceptable, and a spider bite is off limits. I know better now.

Paul leaves the table to photograph the children who've arrived to play their violins. Nikki discovers she's left her headlights on, and Arianna now has her catalyst for leaving Mothering Tea.

In total, I've eaten half a dozen cookies and tarts during this experience. I can feel the sugar in my body. With my head still spinning from the conversation, trying to make sense of what has just happened, I remember a running theme in Dennis' sermons.

The take-home message sinking in is each Sunday, we come together broken, forming the Body of Christ. Our brokenness brings us together, forming a place for new life to emerge. The green shoot emerging from Christ's wound. The seeds germinating only with fire and opening in blackened soil. We are called into a new land, a new home. Mothering Tea may not be this new land, but it's a place to begin. A place of sweet hopefulness. Our desserts, pastel streamers, and mixed tea china are the backdrop to Christian women learning how to be in relationship, in all our colorful, idiosyncratic, mix-and-match brokenness. We are sharing our stories, bit by bit. I'll take that over the social-grace niceties good Southern girls are trained to have. I get to be me even as a priest's wife in this community of independent women and men still drawn together by holy and ancient tradition. What we are creating is yet to be known, but I'm hooked and intrigued. All us sinners are welcome in a place where you're expected to be yourself ten times over. Let the joyful noise begin.

Taste and see that God is good.
—JESC

Joanna's Oatmeal Chocolate Chip Cookie Recipe

½ cup white sugar
¾ cup brown sugar
Cream with 2 ½ sticks of butter
Mix in 1 beaten egg
1 tsp vanilla
½ tsp salt
1 tsp baking soda

2 ¾ cups flour
3 cups rolled oats
1 package semisweet chocolate chips
1 tsp. cinnamon
Dash of nutmeg and cayenne
Once the flour is added, I prefer to mix by hand
Bake 7 to 10 minutes at 375 degrees
Spoon onto an ungreased pan

Clams and Other Mysteries:
10 Stories About Finding Home in the Moment

Are we not in a constant state of traveling from one tiny world to another?

1.

When I was a child on road trips to the Gulf Coast, I often played mind tricks to occupy myself during the ten-hour drive. Particularly on those stretches between Pine Bluff and Lake Providence where rice and cotton fields filled the horizon only to be dotted with the occasional cotton gin or forlorn house, the beautiful melancholy of the land begged for attention. In those moments riding in the family van, my dad at the wheel, my mom listening to a book on tape, my brothers with their headphones on, I stared out the window and looked for an object to let my imagination land on. It might be a rusty lamppost that once served as an important marker for someone's home. Or it could be a faded sign for a Baptist church that may or may not still be in existence. Whatever object I chose, I zeroed in on a tiny space. If I chose the lamppost, I searched for a corner in the black metal, high up near the bulb, and from that space, I imagined myself tiny enough to occupy the corner, and my entire life would be from that perch. The golden light of the bulb would keep me warm in the winter, and I would have cotton fluff for a bed and curtains made out of moth wings. When I lifted the silvery wings, I would see the most beautiful sunsets because it is the Delta, and I would marvel at incredible bird migrations. I would watch the farm equipment scrape away at the land. And I would count the cars zooming by. And from within the comfort of the van, I would think to myself, *I could do that. I would be happy. That could be home.* I only ever scanned the landscape for little worlds that I felt drawn to call home.

2.

We start out tiny and mysterious. Early human civilizations were much less complex, I'm guessing, than our current western day-to-day demands. I look out my office window and see Beacon Hill, Puget Sound, the downtown Seattle skyline, and on clear days, the Olympic Mountains. I wonder about early settlement and the need to survey the land, create maps, draw lines, and delineate boundaries. I am beginning to think the more finely tuned our maps are, the busier our lives become. My favorite pastime in Seattle is to walk the city without a plan or map. The feeling in my body is like caffeine without the jitters. It's the same when I climb the Bitterroots in western Montana. I get to feel tiny.

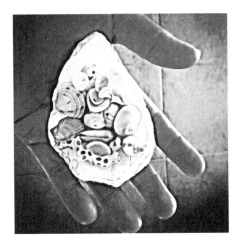

3.
Sometimes I visit the coastlines. When I see a smooth, metamorphic rock on the beach or when I stumble upon massive driftwood the size of dinosaur bones, wonder is my first heartbeat. Swirls are woven in both, and though it's possible to digitally create shapes from nature using the Fibonacci sequence, these swirls have wildness in them. The push and pull of elements twist them into individuals no computer can simulate. I hold the round rock in my hand, and it looks like a small planet, and then I remember we are made of stardust. The rock and I are the same, and the rest is up to mathematicians.

4.
Living in Seattle comes with the unexpected benefit of mouth-watering seafood. Upon arriving here three years ago, a parishioner told us about the best place to get fresh fish and oysters. Esther Mumford thrust a cutout newspaper ad into Dennis's hand at the end of the Sunday service and said, "Here, Father. This is where you want to buy your seafood." Pike Place Market is the known hot spot, and many have seen the bustling open-air market in the film, *Sleepless in Seattle*, where Meg Ryan is sweetly stalking Tom Hanks. Mutual Fish Company, however, is just down the road from us. When you step inside, it's like entering part-ice box, part-aquarium, part-produce (for the ingredients

you may have forgotten like lemons, horseradish, and fresh ginger). Look down into the aerated seawater tanks, and you'll see multiple species of oysters, petite Manila clams, Pen Cove mussels, sea urchins, abalone, and the sci-fi-looking geoducks. Alaskan king crabs rest on ice chips. Chilled cases are full of cod, tuna, salmon, sole, and rockfish. We try to visit as often as possible.

5.
When Dennis was in ICU, our world shrank to the space occupied by beeping IVs, plastic tubes, a breathing machine that almost sounded like ocean waves, hand sanitizer, music, origami sculptures, a globe lamp, leg compressors, yellow gowns, yarn, poetry, and Starbucks cardboard sleeves cut into the shape of hearts and strung together with dental floss. When he woke from the medically-induced coma and began eating and laughing, there was a moment when I thought, *I could do this. This could be our home. We could live in a hospital room forever and be happy.* I told myself this was forever, the here and now. We were so happy. The nurses could hear our laughter from down the hall.

6.
Gratitude List for Sometime in February

Glass pickle jar now filled with wasabi peas on my antique desk.
Thunder, sunshine, and hail out my window while I write.
French press coffee.
Elliot Bay Book Company this afternoon with Dennis.
Lunch at the Mexican place.
Talking about tiny house ideas.
Ridge Fitness across the street.
Hibiscus water.
Granola with yogurt.
A room of my own.

7.
My brother, John, lives in Franklin, Tennessee, on Leanne Way. His home borders a farm, so his kids occasionally find the odd raven-pecked corncob while pretending near the split rail fence. The dried vegetable transforms into an array of imaginary props—one moment the cob is foreign currency only to become a carrier for secret messages before its final resting place as an exotic talisman wrapped in kite string and worn with pride.

8.

On River Ridge Road in Little Rock, Arkansas, my brothers and I were latch-key kids. We lived in an old house built by an apprentice to Fay Jones, who was the apprentice to Frank Lloyd Wright. Its size made it easy to sneak in and out of, but that wasn't necessary until I was a teenager. As young kids, we came and went as we pleased while our parents were star physicians, helping put Arkansas Children's Hospital on the map. I always thought our childhood home looked like Noah's Ark with its twenty-foot arching wooden roof. The floor to ceiling windows led me to pretend our boat was coasting through a glittering canopy of hickory and oak leaves. My dad grumbled over how poorly insulated the house was, how even though it was a work of art, heating and air cost a small fortune. "It's always something with a house," he often says, echoing the lament of his own father. But he bought the house because it is the house my mom fell in love with. She wasn't interested in the traditional colonial brick with the gilded iron door and manicured lawn just up the street.

9.

Email to My Mother During Holy Week

I love you, Mom. I was thinking it would be nice to take a break from Jesus this week. Not the Jesus in my heart but the Jesus Jesus Jesus of organized religion. I'm sure there is a great theological lesson here for me. I'm not really up for knowing what that is at the moment. I helped Dennis reassemble the baptismal font a little while ago. Afterward, I sat in the pew and stared at the reserved sacrament candle. I feel okay in the quiet of the sanctuary—the lit candle—the stations of the cross— purple cloth draped over the crucifix. I picked up the Bible from the pew and began reading Luke. I think Luke is my favorite. How could the Catholics not idolize Mary? It feels sacred and calm sitting in the church alone. I know the congregation is supposed to be the Body of Christ, but I need a break from that particular body. I want the Body of Christ that is quiet and peaceful. I don't even need the promise of Easter. Give me easy breathing and a room of my own while the tide recedes. I know that's only part of the answer. Let me hold off on the other half just for a bit. Maybe my prayer should just be for grace. I keep thinking back to Fat Tuesday. It was a glorious dinner. Shrimp, clams, oysters, cheese, artisan crackers, wine. Don't get me wrong—I understand the necessity of Lent. I even welcome it. It's Holy Week that has me turned inside out.

10.

The Next Day During the Good Friday Service

I sit in the pew and close my eyes. Deep breath. I open my eyes to find all the crosses covered in black. The table bare. Dennis turns the tiny red lights off. As he passes by in his stark cassock, I lean over and whisper, "Even the red lights? Even those?" They're high up and don't put out much light. His nod says, *Yes, even the red lights.*

The reserved sacrament is gone, along with its candle. I feel like I've been punched in the stomach. Some part of me knew this would be gone, but a bigger part of me longed for the sacrament to remain. For the candle to still be there—an eternal flame. *Where is Jesus*, I think. *Where is Jesus in this dark, cold room*?

The day before, I had washed the feet of people I pray with each Sunday. The choir sang the Psalm while the altar was stripped bare. When I heard the cries of counting one's bones, I turned into a snotty, tearful mess. I tried to wipe my face, but the tears kept coming. We left in silence, and I walked home and cried more. Dennis saw me and asked what the matter was.

"I don't like it when the altar is stripped."

"You're not supposed to."

"I know, but it just hurts so much."

He hugged me, and I cried into his shoulder. Blew my nose. A few more tears. Then we ordered pizza from That's Amore across the street.

As the time approaches for the Good Friday service, I begin to wonder if anyone will show up. Then Paul Hill, the Junior Warden, arrives and sits next to me. *Well, I guess it's just us*, I think. We're going to have to see Christ in each other. I can do that. I get what the Bible tells me. But not having the candle and the reserved sacrament makes me realize how much I need to see these artifacts each week. I realize just how much of a Christian I am. It's not enough anymore to experience God in the mountains, to worship at the nature church where I am the only member. And it's not enough to only live a life trying to see Christ's love in each other. I need all of it. I need that candle. I need the church. I need the ritual, the hymns, the prayers, the gathered community, the physical building, and the reserved sacrament. I need the flicker of light that is always burning no matter what is happening in the world or in my life.

After the service, I walk back to the rectory and wipe tears from my face. Dennis begins preparing another meal of clams with garlic. Our Fat Tuesday dinner was so delicious, I had said, "Why do we have to give up this good food up for Lent?"

"You don't," he said, "Why not let that be your Lenten discipline? To enjoy food as a celebration at each meal?"

"That sounds like a good plan," I say.

Feels like home.

Taste and see that God is good.
—JESC

Kinds of Prayer

Knitting.
Making books.
Batiks and writing.
Going to the movies.
Cooking.
Eating Pho.
Compline and morning coffee.

All forms of prayer
for reclaiming meaning.
Healing.
Coming into a new life not
defined by longing
but by abundance.

By grace.

Taste and see that God is good.
—JESC and JJS

Acknowledgments

Grateful acknowledgment to the following publications where stories or earlier versions of stories first appeared:

"Two Scoops," Joanna J. Seibert, *The Call of the Psalms: A Spiritual Guide for Busy People*

"Food at My Grandparents' Table," Joanna J. Seibert, *The Call of the Psalms: A Spiritual Guide for Busy People*

"Coffee with Mary," Joanna J. Seibert, *Healing Presence*

"Coffee in Akron," Joanna J. Seibert, *The Call of the Psalms: A Spiritual Guide for Busy People*

"Coffee in West Point, Joanna J. Seibert, *WomenPsalms*

"Breakfast with Gay," Joanna J. Seibert, *Healing Presence*

"Breakfast with the Osprey," Joanna J. Seibert, *The Call of the Psalms: A Spiritual Guide for Busy People*

"Breakfast at Kanuga," Joanna J. Seibert, *Living Church*

"The Big Spill," Joanna J. Seibert, *Tales from the South Radio Show*

"Revolving Tables Restaurant," Joanna J. Seibert, *The Call of the Psalms: A Spiritual Guide for Busy People*

"Two Parties at Children' Hospital," Joanna J. Seibert, *Healing Presence*